Other Books by *Michael Kluckner*

MICHAEL KLUCKNER'S VANCOUVER
(RAINCOAST, 1996)

THE PULLET SURPRISE
(RAINCOAST, 1997)

CANADA: A JOURNEY OF DISCOVERY
(RAINCOAST, 1998)

WISE ACRES

Free-Range Reflections on the Rural Route

WISE ACRES

Free-Range Reflections on the Rural Route

TEXT AND ILLUSTRATIONS BY

Michael Kluckner

RAINCOAST BOOKS

Vancouver

Raincoast Books acknowledges the ongoing support of The Canada Council; the British Columbia Ministry of Small Business, Tourism and Culture through the BC Arts Council; and the Government of Canada through the Book Publishing Industry Development Program (BPIDP)

FIRST PUBLISHED IN 2000 BY

Raincoast Books
9050 Shaughnessy Street
Vancouver, B.C.
V6P 6E5
(604) 323-7100

www.raincoast.com

Edited by Joy Gugeler
Cover and design by Les Smith
Illustrations by Michael Kluckner

Friends and neighbours appear as characters in a fictionalized form and fictionalized episodes.

1 2 3 4 5 6 7 8 9 10

CANADIAN CATALOGUING IN PUBLICATION DATA

Kluckner, Michael.
Wise Acres

ISBN 1-55192-304-1

1. Kluckner, Michael. 2. Farm life—British Columbia—Langley. 3. Sheep ranchers—British Columbia—Langley—Biography. 4. Farm life in art. I. Title.
FC3845.L35K682 2000   636.3'13'092   C00-910714-2   F1089.L35K68 2000

Printed and bound in Canada

＞—I—◆＞—O—＜◆—I—＜

For Keith Sacré
who encouraged me
and became a true friend

What is this life if full of care
We have no time to stand and stare?
No time to stand beneath the boughs
And stare as long as sheep and cows?
—William Henry Davies
"Leisure"

Contents

><+>—O—<+><

Honk If You Love Peace and Quiet

"How long have you been out there?" Linda asked.

Christine and I were sitting at the dinner table in Linda's elegant city home, the food eaten, the forks and knives together on the plates, a finger of wine left in our glasses.

"It's coming up on six years, six years March the first."

"We were sure you wouldn't last, you know," said Linda. "We thought you'd be back in the city within the year."

"Maybe we'll spend our old age here," I said, "once the work gets too heavy. You know, reverse the trend."

"No regrets? You don't miss being able to drop into a jazz bar on the spur of the moment?"

"Not really. But every once in a while we go to New York or San Francisco to savour the air-conditioning, to feel the concrete between our toes. It's the opposite of holidays in the country, sheep in the fields, roosters crowing."

"Sheepless in Seattle?" Paul, Linda's husband, asked.

"I'm glad *you* said that!"

Linda and Paul had been extremely skeptical about the blood and guts of our farming adventure, but had now developed a grudging respect for the undertaking. Besides, they liked the free-range eggs.

"Maybe it's our age," said Christine, "but we're not spontaneous anymore. We plan a trip to the city like it's a military campaign."

"Besides," I added, "recent outbreaks of spontaneity have left me with a hangover."

Paul rose from the table, picked up a bottle of wine from the sideboard and began to refill the glasses.

"That lack of spontaneity," he said, "is what would bother me about farming, besides the mud and the work. I know we can't just pick up and leave here, either," — he cast a glance around the room, taking in a few valuable paintings, a book-case full of leather-bound volumes, and some small, *very* portable silver sculptures — "but I know how hard it is for you even to go on vacation together."

"True," I said. "The hardest part is getting the sheep seats together on the plane."

"Yeah, right."

"I know I'm defensive about this, but that's always the first question I get asked. I mean, we'll be at a party — always in the city, mind you — listening to someone chattering about his life in refrigerator sales, or whatever, and then he'll ask, 'And what do you do?' I don't want to sugarcoat it, or justify my answer by saying, 'This is our midlife crisis,' or 'We're really doing research for a novel.' I just say, 'We raise sheep and chickens on a little farm.' That's all. And then they'll ask — invariably — 'But how do you get *away*?' This from someone who gets three weeks off a year! They don't say, 'Is it fun?' or 'I bet it smells bad,' or even 'So that explains what's on your shoe.' It's always the same."

"He's exaggerating, of course," said Christine, eyeing my wineglass, and she was right. "My complaint," she said, "is with all those people who've said to me, 'You're from Australia, aren't you? That's why you know about sheep.' I grew up in Sydney, population four million."

>─┼─◆─◆─O─◆─┼─◀

When the 40-something urbanite begins looking for a farm on which to spend his remaining robust years, he is probably far more interested in a picturesque setting than in the quality of the land itself. You could understand this if he was in search of a summer cottage, but if it's a working farm he's after, with healthy crops and sturdy animals, it shouldn't matter a damn what the place *looks* like. But of course it does matter a damn, because for urban refugees farming is more about lifestyle than profit. Indeed, the key is to spend money at a controllable rate, rather like a minor gambling addiction or a hobby such as golf or skydiving; leave profitable agriculture to the factory farmers and multinationals.

In my pre-farming, just-dreaming days, I had imagined a piece of rolling countryside with a mixture of meadows and woods and a view toward mountains, a lake, the sea, something *dramatic*, anything but cul-de-sacs and dream homes, aluminum siding gleaming in the sunshine. I'd enter through a gate off a narrow country road. The rustic driveway, only two gravel ruts with a grassy centre strip, curving through a dappled grove, climbing a hill and emerging into a meadow crested by farmhouse and barn starkly silhouetted against the sky. There would be gables and a deep front porch on which, as in the old saying, "sometimes ah sets and thinks and other times ah jes sets."

There would be a cottage garden for Christine and, in the sunniest spot on the best soil, a big patch of earth for vegetables. The high meadows would be dotted with wildflowers and, of course, my sheep. No slope would be so steep that I'd have to worry about the tractor tipping over to squash me. The woods would be a mixture of conifers and broad-leaved trees shading the forest floor. In the early spring, before the maples and alders burst into leaf, the earth would brighten with crocuses and daffodils. Below the house, just past the edge of the wood, the hillside would drop away to a brook, babbling merrily over stones and moss. We could invite friends over for a weekend to build a weir in the level section, creating a shallow pond to stock with trout. We would get it all done before Miller Time.

Deer would live in the woods and come to the pond to drink in the quiet evening twilight. Rabbits would make burrows under rotting logs...and then reality, usually in the form of a car alarm, would shake me from my reverie.

My city home was on a tree-lined street, venerable and conservative, in a slightly shabby corner of an otherwise-desirable neighbourhood known as Kerrisdale. Detached houses, most of them two-storeyed, with front porches and shallow front gardens, occupied narrow lots. The deep back-yards led to small garages and sheds along an unpaved lane, though most people parked their cars on the street. Our house was a simple frame building, a city cottage, built just before the First World War by a carpenter whose name disappeared forever from the city directory after 1915; likely he took a bullet somewhere in France or Belgium.

Even strangers — a few young mothers pushing baby carriages, old couples out for a stroll in their tired overcoats and hats — were friendly. They stopped to discuss the weather or our garden, chatting in that idle, neighbourly way that was so like living in a village. "Wisteria's really nice this year," they said, referring to the long, purple-flowered panicles that hung among the porch brackets and swarmed up into the high gable every May. "Yes," we agreed. "Those geraniums are sure nice," they said, referring to the pelargoniums in the window boxes along the porch's front rail basking in the summer heat. "Thanks," we replied. Not profound, but polite.

On sunny spring days the neighbour's old mongrel lay on the warm pavement in the middle of the road, twitching now and then as his fleas lunched on him. Only the occasional uptight courier driver disturbed his canine reverie, everyone else willing either to ease past him or to drive around the block.

Christine and I, and our nine-year-old daughter Sarah Jane,

had moved from a comparatively trendy neighbourhood called Kitsilano, which was closer to downtown. After years of Sally Ann furniture and homemade frocks, Christine had decided to put her career back on track and began teaching English at a local college. She was always the one who instigated change. She liked to find an old house that needed work in a neighbourhood just starting to fix itself up, rent out part of it, paint its exterior, strip the ugly wallpaper and remove the Black Sabbath posters, rip up the orange shag and refinish the hardwood floors. Every few years we converted our effort into equity and traded up. She tried to keep us to a five-year plan, the only Stalinist aspect of her character, so we moved on when the renovation was complete and the challenge diminished.

I painted watercolours and exhibited them in a downtown gallery, wrote and succeeded in appearing to all who met me to be both laid-back and easygoing. However, I had my demons: the early death of my mother, who'd enjoyed every moment of her life and deserved a longer one, and the subsequent illness of my father, who'd tried to teach me to save and plan for a comfortable, carefree retirement.

My parents' fate obsessed me. The idea of toiling toward a distant, secure future seemed fruitless. Anyway, I couldn't make up my mind what to do, other than paint and travel and hope that at some point my work too would become the flavour of the month. During his final illness my father grew increasingly convinced that I would become a drifter, but he worried in vain. Christine anchored my rudderless boat: while I was restless, my work like a constant itch that needed to be scratched, Christine managed both to enjoy her work and *thrive* during her weekends and holidays.

I continued to putter, doing my own plumbing, patching and car repairs. Although several times I nearly capitulated, I could never come to terms with the demands of a job at a magazine or an ad agency. In retrospect, a haircut might have done it. If there was a career path I could have followed, I hadn't found the map. But we had modest tastes and expectations and had lived frugally for so long that we weren't able to take pleasure in consumer excess. By comparison, most of my school friends had hopped onto the treadmill and were doing fine, enjoying their purchases and lifestyle without question or cynicism.

In Kitsilano, I had been well disguised among the many artists and writers scratching out a meagre living, earning a few dollars for a drawing here, a few more for an article there, plucking out the first grey hairs and refusing to admit that the world decked itself out in a three-piece suit and charged off to work every morning. I was less anonymous on the Kerrisdale block, where most of our neighbours were seniors tending their gardens and pensions, chatting over the fences, looking out for each other as the years drifted by. From time to time they speculated about how long they'd hang on before selling the house and moving to an apartment closer to the bus stop and the doctor's office. We found our place when just such a person — a widow — put her home on the market after 30 years, years in which she'd done almost nothing to the house beyond planting a cottage garden and adding 12 layers of hideous floral wallpaper. The neighbourhood was prime for an invasion by the younger generation and we were the shock troops.

Nearly a decade earlier, otherwise unemployable, long hair in a ponytail, with an insouciance and a freshly minted university degree, I had delivered mail to houses in this area. Although I'd been a *good* letter carrier and could have used this example of gainful employment to demonstrate to my new neighbours that I really *was* one of them, I kept it a secret. Not because they were retired bankers or lawyers, but because I couldn't recall whether they had fallen victim to my penchant for goading small dogs into ripping up dividend cheques and other valuable mail. I would never have started on such an irresponsible course of behaviour had it not been for a terrier that lurked silently behind one letter slot. With the heavy mailbag over my shoulder and humming the latest Grateful Dead tune, I had ambled up the pathway to the house, climbed its four steps in two strides, bent forward, dexterously flipped open the letter slot and flicked the letters inside. The terrier snatched them from me, pulling so suddenly that my fingers jammed into the narrow opening. There followed a violent ripping, tearing and growling, leaving Her Majesty's Royal Mail in tatters in the vestibule.

Needless to say, this provided an amusing diversion amid the tedium of my rounds. Henceforth, I put cheques on top of other letters, held the wad in my fiercest grip and, when the pooch pounced, tried to drag him muzzle-first through the slot. When I eventually let go, the enraged beast reduced the mail to confetti. Subsequently, the owners installed an outside box and left a nice note explaining their rationale.

With my fun at an end, I began to search for other houses where my footfall sent a chihuahua or poodle into paroxysms of yapping. In short order, by rattling the letters back and forth in the slot and calling, "Here, boy!" into the house, I had trained a few to play my game. The occupants of one of those houses might now be our neighbours. After a particularly vivid nightmare in which I was apprehended, I gave my notice to the postal service and went back to making a living the hard way.

>—⋅⟩⋅⟩⋅⊙⋅⟨⋅⟨⋅—<

A couple of weeks after we moved in, I was disturbed by the ringing of the doorbell. In old jeans and bare feet, carrying a handful of paintbrushes, I opened the door to a middle-aged woman stuffed like sausage meat into a tight suit and nylons. A Welcome Wagon button was pinned to her lapel.

"Is your mother home?" she asked me, obviously perplexed by my appearance.

"You mean my wife?"

She left a brochure and beat a hasty retreat.

So often, you make friends or enemies of your neighbours through your children and your cat. Marjorie (next door) liked Sarah Jane while Tom, her husband, adored Smedley. Beatrice, the widow in the house on the other side of us, was very solicitous of Christine, apparently the Meal Ticket for the whole family.

They were all outwardly, almost rudely, curious about our marriage. Every weekday morning at about eight o'clock Christine emerged from the back door, wearing her power suit and carrying a briefcase, and strode purposefully down the narrow concrete sidewalk to the garage. Barely waiting for the car's oil-pressure light to turn off, she tore down the lane, always a few minutes late. Half an hour later I emerged, wearing old jeans and a sweatshirt, escorted Sarah Jane with her Star Wars lunchbox down the same path, kissed her at the back gate and stood watching until she'd rounded the corner at the end of the lane. Then I shuffled back through the garden toward the house, sometimes distracted by a weed or two, closed the door and reappeared at a back window where I appeared to sit motionless for a couple of hours.

If it were spring or summer, I often ventured out late in the morning and puttered around the garden, sorting the volunteer annuals into neat clumps, hanging obsessively over the erotic petals of a bearded iris. Sometimes, as I sat by the hour in a folding chair, painting the garden or finishing a water-colour, Marjorie threw open her window and called out, "Whatcha doin' today?" "There's a job line out there and you ought to go stand in it," her tone implied. One day, holding a hose to train water onto her nasturtium patch, she asked me to hold up my work-in-progress. "I just don't see how you can fuss over those things for such a long time!" she said. As she got to know me and my books began to be published, she expressed her frustration with the slow pace of my development. "Why don't you write a bestseller?" she asked. One afternoon when we had Marjorie, Tom and Beatrice over for a couple of rye-and-sevens, Marjorie turned sharply to Christine and demanded, "Don't you do windows?" Needless to say, we secretly enjoyed the scrutiny.

When Marjorie and Tom sold their house and moved to a condo, we began to look around. Sarah Jane had, by then, survived her seminal childhood experiences, including repeated strikeouts on the Little League field and concerts of massed ukeleles and flutaphones in the high-school auditorium, so our time was increasingly our own.

As the years went by and our five-year plan stretched into seven years, we too became restless. Sarah Jane had stormed into teenagehood demanding liberation from the parental stranglehold. As my books and paintings sold we ceased to be so dependent on Christine's job. The drudgery of teaching and associated administrative duties was wearing her down and she sought more solace in the garden. We dug up much of the front yard, put in a rockery and planted a low hedge. With each passing season she became further immersed in gardening, interested especially in old garden roses that required more space. Inevitably, she began to contemplate moving to a larger house or, at least, a house with a larger garden.

Unfortunately, city real-estate prices had shot up like a Roman candle.

"What's the point of moving to a bigger place if we have to work even harder to pay for it?" I asked. "More work and less time, especially for you. If you quit, do you think we could get by?" Back to the homemade frocks, perhaps....

The travelling we had done in Europe and Australia had kindled in me an atavistic desire for country life, for the self-sufficiency of a barnyard full of chickens and a big vegetable garden. The more we thought about it, the more we believed we could make ends meet by moving out of the city, simplifying our lives, eating the farm profits and using the art and book revenue for hard currency. After half a lifetime in the city I craved a new experience, something authentic that would infuse my jaded urban soul and reinvigorate my art.

With the omniscience of the teenage race, Sarah Jane cut to the quick. She was just finishing grade 12 and was not about to be uprooted.

"You guys are crazy! What do you want to leave here for? This is a *great* house! It's a *perfect* neighbourhood for you!"

(Translation: "You fit right in with the other old folks and I want you here, should I ever decide to come back.")

"Just because we're adults doesn't mean we're incapable of adventure. Do you think you're the only one with plans?"

"No, but...."

She was desperate to get out on her own. On the other hand, she was more likely concerned that now she'd have to clean her room before moving out. Fortunately, she was able to wangle a scholarship to an Australian university where she could live in residence, but be near her relatives. As eager as she was to split, she realized that if we left this house she might no longer know where home was.

"It sounds like you're retiring," she said wearily, implying we were about to enter our twilight years. "You're too young for that."

"Retirement's too important to leave for your old age," I said, grimly remembering the injustice of my father's early death.

On the autumn day we drove out into the country with a picnic basket and a bottle of wine, we had no intention of looking at hobby farms for sale, but perhaps the wine made us reckless. Was a hobby farm cheaper than a city house? Could we "downsize," and tuck the remaining money safely into Internet stocks or Third World gold mines? One place in particular caught our fancy: a fine old house, its front porch shaded by a huge chestnut tree, on high ground overlooking hedges and pastures. It had a view across rolling countryside toward distant mountains. On a whim, Christine jotted down the realtor's phone number and later gave him a call.

"I've got to be honest with you," he said. "Lotta money and lotta work there. They have permission to subdivide and it's on the edge of the commuter belt."

"Does the price drop further east?" she asked.

"Only a few miles further and you'd notice the difference."

They talked for a few minutes about what was available. Being the practical one, she didn't bore him with my dream of Bambi and the bunnies and a farmhouse under the Big Sky. If I were negotiating, he could have sold us the hobby-farm equivalent of a pig in a poke (an agricultural expression I still don't understand).

"We live on acreage," he told her. "I sell real estate to support my wife's horse habit. The places set up for horses hold their value best. People with lots of money are always moving out from the city, and as women are generally the horse-lovers and call the shots in most families, it's a good bet."

"That's been my experience," she said, chuckling.

He was a good salesman and soon had her talking about what we *might* be interested in: not too heavily treed, southern exposure, five to 10 acres, no bikers within earshot, a house we could fix up, a few farm buildings for the critters, a good well far from feedlots and crops sprayed with pesticides. And cheap. Not a tall order, all things considered.

"I'll keep your name and call you if anything comes up," he said.

"But don't call us with any old place or we'll lose interest," said Christine. "We don't want a stump farm or a place with gravel trucks roaring by all day."

"Okay. Understood."

A couple of months passed, during which we heard nothing and forgot all about the conversation. It was a Saturday morning in early December, the sound of Christmas cash registers jingling in the city air, when he called with news.

"I've just listed a place I think you should see," he said. "There's been some family trouble and the vendor is motivated, if you know what I mean."

"What's the place like?" Christine asked.

"Square property, little house in the middle, old barn, just under 10 acres. Needs work, but not drastic. You could do it gradually."

She looked outside. It was pouring and dreary. The promise of an after-breakfast cat and crossword puzzle in a comfy chair beckoned.

"Do you want to go out to the country to look at a property?" she asked.

"Oh, why not?" I responded halfheartedly.

She turned back to the phone and said, "We can be there in an hour and a half, I guess. What's the address?"

He gave her some numbers and a brief description of the best route. "And you'll see it right away because there's a double row of poplars up the driveway. Looks like a postcard I once saw of France, or maybe it was Italy."

Oh, such fateful words.

An hour later we drove along the main street of a former farming community that had evolved to cater to the overflow of suburbanites, long-distance commuters who wanted cheaper land for a big house or a lifestyle that let a parent stay home with the children. It was a conservative place and, ruefully, we realized it would probably be our local shopping street. No chichi espresso bars or delis with tubs of olives and designer pastas here. We might have to buy a lifetime's supply of parmesan and hoard it for emergencies. A sign outside a doughnut shop read, HONK IF YOU LOVE PEACE AND QUIET. In front of the Hard Times Adult Video Store, a sandwich board declared: WE GIVE YOU MORE BANG FOR YOUR BUCK. Well, maybe it wasn't *that* conservative.

With sinking heart, we turned onto a two-lane road with neat, newly-laid curbs, concrete sidewalks and boulevard saplings. Within a few blocks, though, it dwindled to a country road with gravel shoulders and rough grass. After several more miles we found ourselves near the edge of a very large park. It was raining hard, a degree or two above freezing, and probably as good a time as any to check out a prospective home. After all, if you see it on a sunny day in the middle of summer, don't be surprised when the basement floods in the winter. If you see it on a weekday, don't be surprised when the clown next door gets out his Supertramp albums and barbecues for his baseball team on a summertime Saturday night.

A few minutes later, as we rounded a corner, tall poplar trees came into view. The gate was on a dead-end road that disappeared at a border of trees a few hundred yards farther along. A shiny Mercedes sports car stood in the driveway. This would be the realtor, we cleverly surmised.

My initial impressions of the farm are now a bit of a blur.

We slopped around in the rain, realizing the property was only slightly more interesting, topographically, than a pool table. It was indeed square, 200 yards on each side, sloping gently up from the edges toward the middle. Fences divided it into bare fields with hardly a tree to break the monotony. But it had good bones, including the poplars, the house on the knoll in the middle and a fine old barn. In front of the house, falling away to the south, was a good site for Christine's garden. It was better than any of the other properties we had seen advertised, which were narrow and very deep, meaning that the next-door neighbours, probably including a guy with a big barbecue, would have been right beside us. But there was no winding road, no woodlot, no babbling creek. It was a blank canvas.

Somehow all the shortcomings didn't matter. My dream farm was just that — a dream, like the fantasy in which I move to Tuscany or Provence and restore a derelict but picturesque villa. So what if there was no creek? As a creek is public property, having one would only have meant strangers marching through whenever it suited them, upstream neighbours or their cattle polluting it. So what if the barn needed a roof and some paint? Its ridgeline was still straight. As for the house, well...it could be lived in. Maybe it had good bones too, although it was hard to tell in the rain. Its roof looked fairly new and it had obviously been recently painted. Inside, it was dry and warm. We could fix it up, couldn't we? Without actually committing social suicide by moving farther out to the boondocks, it was as close as I could get to my ideal of living on a property where I couldn't see the smoke from another's chimney. And we would be close enough to the city to sell free-range eggs and organic produce to health-conscious, affluent urbanites!

All the way home we debated the pros and cons. It was stupid, crazy, out of the question and otherwise ill-advised, but we both liked the place and the time was right for a major change.

Back in the city, Christine picked up the phone. We were ready to make an offer.

The ensuing six months passed in a blur. We had offered low and the "motivated" vendors had accepted. It encouraged us that other offers had come in, higher than ours but too late; this news massaged our city egos. We began the round of confessions to our friends.

"You've done *what*?"

"Bought a little farm."

"Whatever for?"

"Well, a change is as good as a rest...."

"So you'll go out there on the weekends, I guess. Have you found a caretaker?"

"Yeah. Us."

At that point, the conversation usually ended.

Our Kerrisdale house sold quickly for — as we had expected — more than the cost of the farm. Fearing we'd be held hostage to a project bigger than anything we had attempted to date, we sought solace in travel through southern Europe for three months, punishing ourselves with trains, airports, lousy restaurant service, pushy strangers with bad breath, diesel trucks, tinny motorbikes, and tiny, smoky hotel rooms with paper-thin walls and saggy beds. So it was that, early in the spring, craving peace and quiet and a little elbowroom, we moved to the country.

THE SHACK

Shelter from the Storm

In the house, in the middle of the almost-featureless green square that was our farm, we unpacked our goods and chattels. As the weather was still blustery and inclement we had plenty of time to take stock, especially when the power blew out and we were reduced to ruminating by candlelight. We retained the curious sensation that we were still travelling, although I had a nagging suspicion that I had lost my return ticket.

After all those nights in strange beds, listening to the sounds of strangers in the next room and to passing cars, the silence here was so deep as to be three-dimensional, drawing us away from the anxiety about our new adventure. Surrounded by our familiar things, but without any hangover of old responsibilities, we slowly began to adjust.

On a whim one day when in the city, I drove down our old block and parked opposite the house. It looked cared for, it and the neighbourhood having adjusted effortlessly to our departure. After sitting there for a minute, I beat a retreat to avoid being spotted by any of our former neighbours. I didn't want them to think I was homesick.

Within a couple of weeks the weather became spring-like and we were no longer waking up in the middle of the night wondering where the hell we were. We spent the days digging Christine's new garden and a large square for vegetables, pushing a wheelbarrow back and forth to an old manure pile left over from the farm's previous life as a cattle feedlot. Gaining in confidence, we began to buy farm animals — four chickens, two geese, two Muscovy ducks, and then, in a giant mammalian leap, five sheep. We were delighted by their personalities and curious habits. Each addition was young and healthy and full of energy. However, *we* collapsed into bed just after sundown with aching muscles, only to be jarred awake by calls from city friends asking, "How's it going? Hey! You sound like you just woke up!"

The house was almost enough to make me a fan of building codes, municipal inspections and other forms of bureaucratic fascism. It was a Cape Cod bungalow, built by someone who had never been to Cape Cod or even seen pictures of it. It was wooden throughout, with horizontal board siding in a style popular in the 1930s, simple single-glazed windows in wooden sashes and an asphalt-tile roof with a gable at each end. It had likely been built by someone who hadn't made anything bigger than a henhouse. Not that I was a connoisseur of fine carpentry, but it was more a shack than a home.

Its lack of quality made me curious, because the barn was a fine old building dating to the beginning of the 20th century, probably constructed from timbers milled on the site when the land was cleared of its original forest. In the weeds and brambles at the top of the driveway, I found a partial answer in two concrete corner posts, broken glass and charred timbers. How close had this place been to the farmhouse in my dream, the one with the gables and the deep front porch? In the damp basement, on a jam-storage shelf, someone had written 1952 RASPBERRY. Some more exploration eventually led to a date, 1951, and an illegible name, scratched in the wet concrete in the corner.

As with any true country property, the house had a well and a septic tank, rather than piped water and a sewer. Although I had never dealt directly with anything other than outhouses and buckets of water from creeks, I understood the principles by which our house operated. Water came from the well, a hole 150 feet deep into the earth, drilled quite recently to replace an ancient hand-dug one near the barn (doubtless a great breeding place for typhoid fever). Its electric pump filled a pressure tank in the basement whenever the level dropped too low; thus it didn't cut in every time you ran the tap for a few seconds.

Before we closed the deal, I had the well's water analyzed at a lab in the city. The computer printout looked like the chemistry test I'd almost failed in grade 12, so I asked the technologist what it all meant.

"No short-term effects!" she cheerily announced.

I smiled wanly.

"Well, there's lots of fluoride, so you can buy cheap toothpaste, and lots of minerals, so it'll keep you regular, and it's okay to drink once you get used to the sulphur smell," she said. "Tell your friends it's bottled Italian mineral water. Buy one of those water-filter jugs and keep it in your fridge."

In the house, the toilet flushed into a septic tank where some of the sludge settled before the remaining *eau de toilette* filtered out into the ground in the septic field through sets of perforated pipes. Where was this septic field? Hard to say exactly, but a big metal pipe below the toilet exited toward the back of the house through the basement wall and eventually, beneath a layer of turf 10 yards behind the house, I found the concrete lid of the septic tank. A tank is supposed to be pumped out every few years or so, but by the thickness of the grass on its lid it hadn't been opened for a decade or more. Best not to look there at all, I thought, and went off seeking something more pleasant to do. Was the grass greener over the septic field? Not really, but at least the septic system was a good 100 yards away from the wellhead.

The real curiosity was the grey-water system. In a rural house, grey water is what isn't polluted (unlike blackwater — toilet flushings) but obviously isn't clean. The water from the sinks and shower does contain some dirt, but in theory doesn't need to be percolated into a septic field. I became curious because I couldn't see where the kitchen sink drained; it just seemed to go into the concrete floor in the basement. In the city, it goes into the sewer and then it's the city's problem — you pull the plug and it's gone. But in the country you dispose of all your liquid waste on your own property, which could mean you're operating a diner for every rat in the vicinity.

In one gloomy corner of the basement, far from the glaring light of an exposed 60-watt bulb, there was a ragged, water-filled hole in the concrete floor, about six inches deep. This was the sump, keeping us from a flood during heavy rains and snowmelts. Standing in the middle of the hole was a large pump, a contraption about a yard tall with an electric motor on top, from which two wires emerged, attached with electrician's tape to the chopped-off end of an extension cord that plugged into an outlet on the wall.

Below the motor was a shaft that disappeared into the dark water, at the bottom of which was presumably the pump itself. A taut cord connected a lever to a rubber weight floating in the water; when the water level in the sump rose, the weight would rise too, releasing the pressure that kept the lever — the switch — in the "off" position. A thick black plastic pipe emerged from a connection on the side of the pump. My eye followed it to the basement ceiling, where it was tied to a joist with some baler twine, then along to a small window just below ceiling level where, through a knocked-out pane, the pipe disappeared into the backyard. The setup reminded me of a VW Beetle I had once had, so simple mechanically that even I could understand how it worked, but so deteriorated that it was impossible to maintain.

As I absorbed the sump pump's workings, I heard rattling and crashing in the kitchen above. Christine was at the sink, running water and washing breakfast dishes. The sound of the plug being pulled and the rush of descending water was followed a few seconds later by bubbling in the sump. I peered into the blackness and could see oily water containing toast crumbs rippling upward and raising the grubby little rubber weight. The cord slackened and suddenly the pump kicked into life, forcing a pulse of dirty water through the black pipe and outside. I ran for the basement stairs and headed around the back to where the pipe emerged. Tracing it through the long grass toward a gurgling sound, I found the spot where it emptied. A slurry of food bits, soap and grease stained the lush grass. It reminded me of descriptions of medieval Europe shortly before the arrival of the bubonic plague, when towns-people routinely threw their slops out onto the street.

"Back-to-the-land" books advise you to channel all your grey water toward your vegetable garden and somehow feed it into ditches between rows of plants, where it can fertilize the soil while saving clean water for other purposes. My first thought, however, was to make sure it didn't back up and flood the base-ment. Every time we finished the dishes and drained the sink I would listen intently to hear the sump pump start; if it didn't, perhaps because it had clogged with slime and popped the circuit breaker, I would rush downstairs to try to get it going. Sometimes I'd have to bail the sump into a bucket and toss it out onto the grass myself. Ah, the pleasures of country life!

As the months went by, I found other delights for the senses and challenges for the pocketbook as well. An addition on the side of the house had been erected without the bother of a proper foundation. Now it was settling, falling away from the main structure, and opening a gap into which snow melted and rain dripped. What had appeared to be a fresh coat of paint on that dreary December day when we first saw the house was just that: new paint slapped over old paint that had begun to peel and flake, largely because the siding was rotting underneath due to the humidity in the walls. In May, the sunny side of the house became absolutely covered with mating flies. For a couple of weeks, friends who called up and wanted to drop by on a Sunday drive in the country were given the brush-off. Even in the most manure-strewn portion of the barnyard you could enunciate your words properly without fear that flies would pop into your mouth, but it was a different matter at the house. We began to suspect a corpse in the attic, the existence of which perhaps had precipitated the sale of the farm.

The house also had chronic electrical problems — switches that worked only in wet weather, weird connections inside switch boxes, bare wires held together by plastic tape. I was terrified to touch any of it, sure that if it was disturbed at all it would vindictively catch fire and incinerate us while we slept. On the bright side, the house had beautiful wooden floors made of strips of tongue-and-groove fir that were warm underfoot. It also had front sliding doors that opened onto a ground-level deck.

Eventually, we rounded up the money and the will to make some improvements. I had hoped to hoard the profit from the sale of the city house for our toothless old age, but Christine was unwilling to live the rest of her days in a hovel. Accordingly I phoned Donna, a friend from the city who was a general contractor, and invited her and her husband Philip to dinner. Curious to see what kind of mess we had gotten ourselves into, she readily agreed to advise.

Donna moved slowly around the house, peering into corners with a flashlight, occasionally jabbing at pieces of wood with a screwdriver. She didn't say much or offer many opinions as we toured, listening instead as we babbled along happily about this room becoming bigger or the next one smaller, a window to be put in here and so on. Finally we returned to the kitchen and began to drink in earnest as we awaited her verdict.

"Except for under the living room, the foundation's solid. You could keep that."

"And what about lifting the roof at the back to expand the bedrooms upstairs?"

"Don't even think about it," she said. "Keep the concrete foundation walls and build on them. There isn't enough solid wood in this place to roast a bag of marshmallows."

"So we start over?" Christine asked, stating the obvious.

"You'd be throwing good money after bad if you tried to fix this place up. And as soon as you started to renovate, the permit police would come down on you like a ton of bricks and make you completely redo that basement plumbing. You'd have to start over anyway."

With that decided, life suddenly seemed simple. We had dinner and spoke of other things.

Before Donna's visit, we had been preparing ourselves psychologically for the kind of slow, steady renovation — in reality a prolonged disruption — that taxes even the best marriage. Neither of us had any idea whether building a new house would be any easier. If we were to build, we were *really* committing ourselves to the rural life. Alas, my Plan B — muddling along with the sump pump and the eccentric wiring — had received no spousal support. Although I don't recall that we discussed it, after a year on the farm we seemed to be content enough to invest and improve for the long term.

Donna had left with some final advice: build a cottage (which was all we wanted and certainly all we could afford); don't build unneeded bedrooms, because relatives will want to visit or children move home (actually, this was my interpretation); build only on one level, because it will be easier to move about in your wheelchairs once the farmwork beats you into submission (ditto); draw the plans yourselves and hire a building student to redraw them to the building code; hire a local project manager to build the house; and finally, don't leave the property while construction is under way if you want to make sure they do it *your* way. Above all, she repeated, keep it simple.

"I couldn't get over the size of the places we drove past on the way out here," she told us. "Ride-on lawn mowers outside and ride-on vacuum cleaners inside. You don't need that kind of maintenance. You'd be more tied down than if you had live-stock!"

We smiled politely.

"People always carry on about *resale*," said Philip. "They build with the idea of selling it down the road, rather than living in it now."

"I don't think we could live in the sort of place that would be appealing for resale anyway," said Christine, having arrived at certain conclusions about the tastes of the country gentry.

"Do you know anybody who has a trailer or an RV?" Donna asked. "You could live in that while you build."

"Doubt it, but we'll think of something," said Christine.

I had been reflecting on articles in cottage magazines, wherein the fearless chartered accountant forsakes his spread-sheets for a hammer and a saw.

"If we made it really simple, do you think we could build it ourselves?" I asked Donna.

"In your dreams."

"By the way," said Philip, "I read an article in a business magazine about a company that's doing computer-assisted manufacturing. You draw your plans to scale, they digitize them and prefabricate the walls of your house in their factory. Then you just have to hire somebody to nail it together and do the plumbing and electrical and you can finish it yourself. That might be worth investigating."

My first impression of the farm — a blank canvas — was truer now than ever. Drawing on my vivid memories of Drafting II, I began by measuring the rectangular foundation and then copying the dimensions of rooms in friends' houses we liked. We also measured key pieces of furniture, like the bed and dining room table, and fitted rooms around them. Christine wanted a walk-in pantry off the kitchen. When people came over they spent all their time in the kitchen and dining room anyway, so we made the living room no bigger than a nook with space for a couch, bookshelves and a cabinet for stereo and TV. We had enough area to run the kitchen and the dining room together, with space between them for a couple of chairs where people could sit and talk with us while we cooked. If we had all the relatives out for Christmas dinner, we could add tables and seat everyone in boardinghouse style. The freestanding woodstove would go in the seating area between the kitchen and the dining table, where it would heat the house on even the coldest winter days. There was no need for a rec room, as we knew we would have little, if any, recreation. One big bedroom for us, a bathroom and a tiny second bedroom completed the rectangle.

We loved the houses of the Australian Outback, crouched protectively against the harsh climate, and thought ours might look similar. They have verandahs that run the length of their façades and tall, pyramidal metal roofs — at least as tall as the walls — that collect rainwater for a tank. The pronounced overhang shelters the interior from the fierce sun. We would need that for the summer, but around the time of the fall equinox the sun would be low enough in the sky to creep into the house through the French doors we planned to put on its front façade. By midwinter the low sun would stream all the way in and warm the interior, but wind-borne rain would not splatter so hard on the windows. In late May, when the heat returned as the sun climbed in the sky, the rays would be blocked by the eaves and the interior would stay cool.

And why not build it ourselves? Perhaps Christine and Donna were unnecessarily dismissive of my latent carpentry genius. A myriad of magazine articles read over the years implied that it was not only possible, it could also be a life-affirming experience, an opportunity to nest while confirming the unbreakable bond with one's spouse! Hmm ... Christine and I had once built a picket fence together and argued for weeks afterward. Besides, there were practical concerns, even more important to us than the survival of our marriage. We *weren't* far from marauding building inspectors. We *did* need it to pass inspection, if for no other reason than to get electricity hooked up and the contents insured. Furthermore, I had heard that the township demanded a house be finished within six months from the time it issued the permit. Do-it-yourself was out of the question.

As we mulled over the possibilities, we tried to determine where we were going to live while the new place rose from the ashes of the old. We didn't know anybody with a mobile home bigger than a Volvo station wagon. At night, the barn was a war zone of feral cats competing for turf or hunting the rats and mice that lived in deep burrows under the floor. Another disincentive was its shrieking barn owl and her babies — a sound somewhere between that of nails-on-a-blackboard and ripping canvas. The mother owl returned from the fields between dusk and dawn with fresh voles to disembowel for dinner.

But there *was* a building that offered some promise of temporary accommodation and, later, could provide guest quarters. At the top of the driveway was a big equipment shed, badly deteriorated, awaiting a windstorm to push it onto its back. It was three bays wide, each one large enough for a big tractor. Two of them were open-fronted, but the third had been closed in. It had a couple of windows on the side and a top-hung, sliding door, so it served as a toolshed. However, it did have an airtight stove and a metal chimney that poked through its tin roof.

Perhaps this was the home *I* could build! After surveying the situation and consulting Chuck, the neighbour whose field was across our back fence and who seemed a practical chap, I gingerly mounted a ladder and cut through the roof with a chainsaw, separating the open bays from the toolshed. To my chagrin the orphaned bays merely slumped backward into a sulk, but didn't actually fall flat, leaving an even-more-dangerous "widowmaker." Chuck obligingly brought over his biggest tractor, pushed them over and heaped the rubble. Before he went home, I tied the strongest rope I could find to the centre vertical stud in the toolshed and had him pull the building upright. Old wooden buildings can be very flexible.

To turn the shack into a home, we cashed in all the chips in order to attract a labour supply. Laying in quantities of beer and pizza, we got a work party together and managed, on a long, sunny Saturday in May, to put in some wood-framed windows we'd found in the barn, replace the door with one from the local flea market and sheathe the newly exposed bits of the shed's exterior with siding ripped off the doomed Cape Cod. In one corner we partitioned off an area for the bathroom and installed a Swedish composting toilet, the type that's advertised to cottagers as FREE TOILET WITH PURCHASE OF SAAB TURBO, and the bathroom sink from the house. Plywood nailed onto the interior walls stiffened the structure and reminded me of the "rustic" summer cabin I recalled from my childhood. The resulting abode was as big as a motel room, about five by six yards, and couldn't possibly be construed by the building inspector to be an attempt to create a second dwelling on the property. Sharecroppers' cabins in the Deep South were more palatial. Once we'd hooked up a hose to the sink we'd be ready to camp for the duration of the project.

>-+-+>-+-O-+<+-+-<

I had seen too many houses under construction, sheathed in chipboard and framed with fingerjointed studs, that looked as if they were being built from scrap. There was a better chance of quality control if we could find the right company. A few inquiries led us to the firm that did computer-assisted manufacturing. Even the roof was easily done that way, with trusses manufactured off-site and delivered to the farm on the back of a truck. A student who had worked for the company the previous summer redrew our plans, filling them with neatly printed specifications and checking the room sizes against the building code. Everything from the metal roof to the board-and-batten cedar siding to the wood-sashed windows was of high quality, affordable because the house was so small — about 1,200 square feet.

With the rolled-up plans under my arm, I chugged up the road to the township hall to present them to the functionary behind the building-permits counter.

"Haven't seen one this small for a long time," he said laconically. But he was friendly and I'd caught him on a slow day. "Aren't you worried about resale?"

"I plan on dying here," I replied, "so it won't be my problem."

"Matter of fact, I think you're smart," he said. "We've got too many bedrooms now the kids are gone, but we don't want to move."

The fact that the house was being engineered and prefabricated made it easier for the powers that be to approve. Two days later, after handing over a $1,000 deposit, reading fine print and signing umpteen forms, we had the permit.

But my town-hall acquaintance's easygoing manner of the previous visit had vanished. Pointing to a spot on the form, he said, "You're not allowed to move in until we've issued an occupancy permit."

"No problem," I answered blithely.

Evidently the local government was determined to control do-it-yourself builders. A generation earlier there had been a do-as-you-please attitude toward construction and building codes that fitted the rural nature of our immediate surroundings. But this attitude was also responsible for allowing the Cape Cod to become a junker in the first place.

As I walked away with my permit and approvals I recalled a story one of our country neighbours (a longtime resident) had told me. New to the area, he had gone to the township hall to file paperwork for a cabin. The fire chief was responsible for issuing building permits.

"The cabin'll be just over 400 square feet," my neighbour said.

"We don't require permits for any building under 400 square feet," replied the chief.

"Yes, but mine will be just *over* 400 square feet."

"I think you should remeasure it."

He got the hint. Saying he'd be back, my neighbour walked across the street to a coffee shop where he whiled away a half hour chatting up the waitress before returning. The chief was still there, killing time until the next big fire.

"I rechecked my plans and it's just under 400 square feet," my neighbour announced.

"Good," said the chief, smiling. "I won't need to issue a permit then."

>─┤◆──○──◆├─<

Donna had suggested we hire a project manager who knew the local tradesmen and had the clout to get them to the construction site on time. There was no point in, for example, having a cement truck arrive in the driveway if the forms weren't ready because the framer was at home nursing a hangover.

Ken was a big, bluff character with a cheerful face who had done some work in the past for the prefab company. His career had been spent defacing the countryside with hideous suburban houses with double-height entryways, neo-Palladian windows and vinyl siding in subdivisions called "Brandywine," more aptly named "Rum 'n' Coke."

He brought with him an envelope of photographs of his past efforts. We nodded and murmured insincere compliments. At least they *looked* well built. Ken was as intrigued by us as we were by him. He examined the house design with a practised eye, drawing conclusions about how we lived. Evidently he was very hands-on and determined to do our bidding. More than just managing, he would be working as one of the crew of carpenters assembling the house. He assured us he knew a good plumber and electrician and had worked with other tradespeople we would need to get the job finished.

"You just gotta ride 'em," he declared. "They're all good people, but they got no sense of time."

"Well, that'll be your job — we want to be able to move in by the middle of October."

"Some of the people I've worked for take off while we work — they can't stand all the dust and commotion."

Donna's warning — to stick around for the many on-the-spot decisions — had to be heeded. Anyway, where would we go? Where could we *afford* to go?

"No, we'll stick around," I said.

"But where are you gonna stay?" he asked, glancing over the property.

"In the shack over there!" I announced proudly, gesturing toward my picturesque hovel.

"Nah ... lemme see this," he exclaimed. He marched toward it on his thick, long legs; I had to run to keep up. Ken went from 0-60 almost instantly. He thundered right up to the shack and ploughed through the door.

For a moment he surveyed the unfurnished space, pulling at the corner of his moustache. I watched him, noting that, although the weather was quite cool, he was wearing shorts and a T-shirt. Fuelled by Pepsi and sandwiches, his boiler ran hot.

"Okay, so where's the shower?"

"Uh, well, we're going to get one of those solar shower kits you can buy at camping stores." He began to frown. "You know, you fill it with water and leave it out in the sun for the day." His frown deepened. "We had one when we used to go camping and it worked well too, until the squirrels ate it."

"Lookit, I'm going to fix you up before you move in," he announced, whipping out a tape measure and marching into the partitioned-off bathroom area.

Without having figured out a detailed plan, we nevertheless agreed that everything would start in the first week in June. "Everything" included moving out of our pathetic house so it could be demolished. There was plenty of room in the old horse stalls in the barn for all the tables, chairs and boxes of books that wouldn't go into the shack. With some tarps and a couple of blocks of rat poison, our belongings would be safe for the summer.

While we were still in the process of carting boxes to the barn, I put an ad in the local paper offering the house for salvage. One couple came by and unscrewed a few of the old electrical fixtures and another took some of the windows for a greenhouse. I removed other windows for an upgrade to the henhouse; as they were not double-glazed, they didn't meet the building code so couldn't be reinstalled in the new house. After we had stripped all the usable siding from the exterior to resheathe the shack, there was little left of any value, except the fine fir flooring we wanted to reuse. I went to town and found a cabinetmaker to ask for advice.

"Ease the boards up with wedges," he told me. "Work along slowly from one end to the other to ease them off their finishing nails."

I started in the main bedroom, where the floor was least worn, prying slowly from the corner. The first board split. Thinking I was too anxious, I slowed down. Then the second board split. Impatient, I jacked it up and discovered it was nailed with a common nail, the kind with a big flat head. The builder had probably been too lazy to get finishing nails and just used what he had.

I phoned a man who had wanted to buy the floor and explained the problem. Later that day he showed up with his wedges and tools. He worked until midnight trying to salvage the strips, but it was hopeless. He settled for a few doors and miscellaneous pieces of wood and finally, after falling down the partially demolished basement stairs, went home, depressed. We had recycled what we could.

Chuck, who had been following the process over the fence, ambled over the next day to inspect what was happening. The gutted house, with half its siding removed and ragged sheets of tar paper flapping in the breeze, was a classic rural eyesore. With the addition of Daisy Mae and Pappy and Mammy Yokum, it would have made a convincing set for a movie version of *Li'l Abner*.

"Got any old beaters you want to park in front?" I asked Chuck.

"No, I'm just checkin' up on you," he said with a grin. "How're you gettin' rid of it?"

"Can't afford to," I said, enjoying the look of panic that crossed his face. "The project manager we hired is going to make all the arrangements."

"You could always burn it down — save yourself the dump fees."

"That would pollute."

"The guy who lived here before you used to say that anything you burn at night doesn't pollute. That's when he burned his old horse blankets."

A couple of days later, Ken arrived in a rusting ex-postal van with HARRY'S PLUMBING hand-lettered on the side. The driver was a balding, middle-aged man with shoulder-length hair whom Ken introduced as Harry, his brother-in-law and our plumber. If he didn't have anything to say he didn't say anything, and his T-shirt needed a wash, but Harry was an agreeable sort. He gave new meaning to the word *taciturn*, while Ken was voluble and funny. I wondered what other relatives I would meet during the construction.

Ken opened the back doors of the van and began to haul out a fibreglass shower stall. Harry shuffled over to help him, and together they got it upright in the dusty driveway.

"What's this, then?" I asked.

"Guy at the local wholesaler owed me a favour. It's a second, so I got it for nothing. Harry had a little water heater in his garage so we'll put that in too. Hunnerd-ten volt, so you won't have to rewire."

"Where?"

"In your cabin!" he grinned, jerking his head in the direction of the shack. "Meanwhile, I gotta figure out how much drywall there is in the old house before I can get a crew in to remove it."

"Why?"

"You can't dump drywall in the landfill. Releases hydrogen sulphide — you know, smells like rotten egg. It's gotta be recycled."

Ken and Harry went off together to reconnoitre the shack. A few minutes later they were back at the van, removing the water heater. Harry unloaded a toolcase and a roll of plastic plumbing pipe from the truck and disappeared inside again.

"C'mere," Ken ordered and bounded over to the side of the shack. "We're going to build a shower enclosure here. Can't put a doorway from inside so you'll have to walk around. We'll just leave it open" — he gestured across our back field to the distant vineyard — "so's you can enjoy the view. Okay? You got any old lumber and plywood around here?"

I pointed toward a woodpile near the barn, which included the stuff I'd been able to salvage. A few minutes later he was back, carrying an armload of 2 x 4s and other scraps. Putting on his leather carpenter's belt and unloading power tools from the back of Harry's van, he set to work in a flurry of sawing and hammering. In a matter of minutes the scraps became walls with a roof atop them. Harry emerged from the shack and helped manoeuvre the fibreglass shower stall into the enclosure, then snipped and clipped pipes together to connect it to the water heater he had been installing on the other side of the wall.

Obviously pleased with their work, Ken beamed and Harry smirked. I got the impression that this was all under the category of "establishing good customer relations," so there would be no bill. Ken just wanted us to be comfortable during what he knew, better than we, would be a long and arduous process.

As they were about to leave, I asked Ken if he'd help me remove a heavy gate from a fence beside the house. It was left over from the farm's previous life as a cattle operation. Christine and I had wrestled it, with much sweating and cursing, onto the pin hinges when we first moved in. I dashed into the house to grab a pair of gloves, but when I returned I found Ken holding the gate in his bare hands as if it were made of bamboo. "Okay," he said. "Where do you want it?"

>-+◆>-◦-<◆+-◄

A couple of days later the troops arrived. A pickup truck that looked as though it had come second in a demolition derby appeared at the bottom of the driveway. On its bed a hand-built box had been erected, using scrap lumber. JAKES DEMOLITION and NO JOB TOO BIG were hand-lettered on the sides in red paint.

Two rough-looking, unshaven men with lank black hair emerged and began to unload what looked like burglary tools. The tall one, distinguishable from his partner because his jeans were ripped only in one knee, tied a kerchief over his coif, giving him a vaguely piratical air, and acknowledged my presence with a gesture toward the derelict house. "Here tah do dah gyproc," he mumbled. At least I think that's what he said.

"You Jake?" I asked.

"No, I'm Brian."

The short one made a beeline for the interior and, quickly locating his prey, began to whale away at the walls.

A cacophony of banging and crashing followed. Periodically, puffs of dust wafted from the holes in the walls and chunks of drywall sailed out and landed around the perimeter. After a couple of hours the racket ceased, so I left my task in the barn and walked back to the house to see how they were doing. Brian, now powdered as white as a mime, was standing at the window and smoking a cigarette. In the background I could hear his partner coughing and hacking, as if he and his lungs were about to part company.

"Shouldn't you be wearing a mask?" I asked. (I could have added, "and does your mother know you smoke?") I was afraid he'd claim a work-related disability and sue.

"Too hot today, can't get enough air," he said in a voice that sounded like gravel being stirred in a tin bucket. "Jacques there," — he gestured over his shoulder with the cigarette to where his partner was still wheezing — "won't wear one cuz he likes the voice it gives him. He sings in a punk band on weekends."

Several hours later they had all the gyproc out on the grass and were chucking it into the back of the pickup. The recycling depot was paying for gyproc now, Brian grinned, so they'd get an extra case of beer for their day's work. I went inside, picking my way across the dusty floor through the mess of boards and nails left from the salvage attempt. He followed in order to point out a panel beside the kitchen stove that had slices of red brick glued to it — a *faux* chimney, one of the charming features of our country kitchen that would have impressed Martha Stewart.

"That's not wallboard, man, that's asbestos. We can't touch that."

"Why?"

"Too dangerous. We lose our insurance if we touch asbestos unless we get suited up and use respirators," he croaked in his dust-ravaged voice.

"Well, what am I going to do with it?"

"Your call, man. You can hire a special crew. Whatever. But it's against the law to demolish a house with asbestos in it."

I paid their invoice and they were soon on their way. The following morning, rigged up in my best approximation of a space suit, I gingerly pried the panel off the wall, wrapped it in plastic and drove it to the toxic-waste dump. Now, finally, the place could come down.

At 5:30 a.m. we were awakened by a racket at the end of the driveway. Squinting, with bleary eyes, through the window I could see a huge excavator — the kind of contraption used to demolish heritage houses in the city — being unloaded from a low-bed truck. A few minutes later, the driver had parked it by the house and departed.

At 7:30 a.m. Ken arrived with his crew. In about an hour the husk of the house was flattened and an enormous truck arrived, pulling a trailer painted in the colours of the Union Jack and emblazoned with the letters BIG BIN. As it was too big to make the corner, Ken and one of his men removed the gate and a few posts. By midafternoon the rubble was gone. The excavator worked on, cutting away the earth around the old foundation so that proper drain tiles could be installed, digging trenches for water and power lines and a deep pit for the new septic tank. By dusk, everyone had gone and we were left alone in the shack.

Christine and I had by this time settled in happily, cooking on the barbecue or on a Coleman stove left over from an ancient road trip, showering *en plein air* with the view of the vineyard. The weather was hot and dry and stayed that way for weeks.

For several days after BIG BIN, very little happened. A load of lumber was delivered and Ken dropped by once and ran around with his tape measure. Then, one morning, he arrived with two carpenters and in a day they built the floor. Another pause followed, during which we tended the garden and puttered around with the farm tasks, interrupted only by the arrival of a large truck with a hoist that unloaded the wall sections. A day or so later Ken and the crew came back and in a 12-hour marathon, fuelled by gallons of Pepsi, they erected all the outside walls and built the inside ones using the pile of 2 x 4s lying in the dust. At the end of the week the large truck with the hoist reappeared and unloaded the roof trusses in bundles atop the walls, where they were easily positioned and secured. By the time the metal roof went on and the windows were fitted, there had been only one thunderstorm to knock the dust down and it was already the middle of August.

And so, a bit at a time, in fits and starts, our dream cottage took shape. We knew we were on the right track the day that Karen and Keith, who had moved to the country years before we did, arrived in the driveway in a cloud of dust. Keith looked at the framed-in house and recited the opening words from Isak Dinesen's *Out of Africa*: "I had a farm in Africa...."

However, the closer we got to finishing the house, the more our project began to fray at the edges. Everything we wanted met with opposition from tradesmen. I got the feeling they'd been installing aluminum windows and vinyl siding for so long that they had no sense of how wood ought to be handled. "It'll cost more," was a constant refrain. The drywaller, a German emigré who took himself very seriously, was offended when we said we didn't want a textured ceiling.

As the house approached completion — at least in a structural sense — Ken's job neared its end, but he continued to buzz around conjuring up tradesmen who could put up siding, lay down floors and do the finishing work the place needed to make it habitable. Costs for the cedar boards we wanted for the exterior were exorbitant. Finally, after listening to one too many prospective installers, I announced to Ken that I was going to finish the place myself. Taking pity on me (and probably wondering whether I needed an Excedrin), he lent me his table saws and pneumatic nail gun so I could become "a real carpenter." Based on observations of their behaviour, I began drinking gallons of Pepsi, adding tooth decay to my list of anxieties.

The work was slow but satisfying. I was grateful that it was just a bungalow, the highest point on the walls only eight feet off the ground. Through September and into the early weeks of October we laboured. Christine found an old tool cabinet in the barn and refinished it as a bathroom vanity. She painted the inside of the house and the outside window frames. Harry returned and hooked up all the taps and sinks. Ken came back one last time and helped me install the woodstove.

We stayed on in the shack, with tomatoes ripening on all the windowsills and the stove burning at night, working long hours every day to finish the interior. The trip outside to the shower became increasingly bracing. We were tired of building, tired of all the detail and the decisions, but felt at least that we had come as close as we could to building our own place.

Our folly now needed a name: "Wiseacres" seemed clever, but it probably wouldn't wear well. Eventually, we agreed on "Killara Farm" after the neighbourhood in Sydney where Christine had grown up. In aboriginal dialect, it meant "stay forever" or "never be able to leave," both of which seemed appropriate.

In late October, four and a half months after we had left the old house, we moved into the almost-finished new one. All around its perimeter were gouges and ruts where a backhoe had installed the concrete septic tank, where trenches had been backfilled and grass and plants crushed by piles of lumber and too many booted feet. But the trees around the house had survived, their leaves golden and crimson in the bright autumn sun.

I walked outside one afternoon and was overwhelmed by the certainty that *this* was really home, that we had made it ours with our sweat and our fortune. Irrevocably, we had started a new chapter, leaving behind any thoughts of returning to the city. Christine saw me gazing in the slanting sunlight, stopped what she was doing and came out to stand beside me. As we stood together admiring our new home, she took my hand in hers.

Eventually I spoke. "I want to be buried here," I told her.

She said she was too busy to do it, so we went inside and got back to work.

A Ruminant of One's Own

Call it beginner's luck, but our first lambing season was a stellar one. We had purchased four Romney ewes and a ram earlier, named, respectively, Gladys, Mary, Norah, Jenny and Eric — collectively known as the Gang of Five. They were, apparently, healthy and trouble-free and produced nine lambs. What's more, I avoided getting T-boned by Eric during breeding season.

I was sure raising sheep would be easy because Chuck and Angela's flock, which paraded from paddock to pasture as if on a streetcar track, appeared to require little care. We were happy we had chosen Romneys, as their wool was long and lustrous and in demand by spinners and weavers. Our sheep thus had a practical use beyond providing dinner and lawn order.

Gladys, an easygoing ewe with a beautiful fleece, had two strong lambs, a boy and a girl, followed by a runt that she rejected and forced us to raise as a bottle lamb. Jenny, a more skittish sheep, decided to give birth in the field during a sleet storm. She produced the first lamb successfully, but then had trouble with the second, obliging me to prove that my long thin hands were more than merely a symbol of my patrician ancestry. No sooner had I delivered the second lamb, steaming in the cold air, than Jenny produced a third. For a moment, as we both rested from our labours, I contemplated a guest appearance in "All Creatures Great and Small."

That first spring, Christine and I were still undecided about a critical issue in hobby farming: to name or not to name. Everyone, even a city person, understands the truism that it is harder to eat a named animal than an anonymous one. A bit of a chill falls over a dinner party when the lamb roast, carved and arranged on a platter, is placed on the table and some wit asks, "So who's this, then?"

Thus we named only the firstborn boy and the girls we planned to keep as we built our flock — someday there would be enough sheep for any insomniac to count. We did, however, clip coloured and numbered tags onto their ears so we could tell mothers from daughters as they matured. It was important to identify the right bloodlines if we wanted to develop and reinforce certain attributes.

Gladys had her lambs on the day our friends Eliza and Edward married, so that took care of names for the two strong ones, and the bottle lamb, dear little soul that she was, was named Snurgle — Snurg for short. Snurgle took her name from the sound her mouth made as she sucked on the rubber nipple stretched over the rim of a beer bottle filled with goat's milk. A bottle lamb is very useful when you're just starting out on a farm and your city friends have taken a break from shopping to troop out and see how you're doing. Like a magician, you clap your hands and out of the pasture bounds a woolly, bright-eyed creature about the size of a spaniel. Unlike normal lambs, a bottle lamb's instinct to flee is suppressed. Being held and stroked has the same effect on them that a nudge or a lick has on normal lambs. Bottle lambs have a way of making erstwhile serious adults — even ones like me who can't look at human babies without wondering whether they'll grow up to be mass-murderers — misty-eyed and sentimental.

Anyway, enough about their cuteness, for to the practical shepherd they're a nuisance, requiring middle-of-the-night feeding and other special care. Not surprisingly, old-time countrymen often killed them at birth as it is very difficult to give a lamb to another ewe to raise. Ewes know exactly who's who, by smelling their own milk as it exits the other end of the lamb, and will push away any lamb that's not their own.

The how-to, ewes-are-friendly sheep books are full of advice on orphan-adoption strategies, usually involving restraining the ewe for 48 hours or smearing the lamb with the amniotic fluid of the "receiver" mum. Shepherds in the Scottish Highlands skin any dead newborns and keep the pelts to use as costumes for orphans. Hens, by contrast, will sit on anybody's eggs and accept any chick as their own. Farmers who keep dairying breeds such as East Friesians, usually for cheese-making, raise all their lambs on the bottle, removing them from the ewes after two or three days and feeding them cow's milk. Often the farmer will keep a Jersey cow, which produces milk with a higher fat content than the standard dairy Holstein. The warm milk is poured into a special bucket with several rubber teats protruding from it. Each lamb returns religiously to its "own" teat, just like twins who prefer one side of their mother over the other. Elsewhere in the world, for example in the region of southern France where Roquefort cheese is produced, a thriving "kid"-glove business has developed due to the proximity of the cheese industry!

Mary, the leader of the flock, had a girl and a boy that first year. As I recall, the boy got barbecued and the girl got the clever name Mary's Girl. Norah, the most phlegmatic of the flock, the sort of sheep you could count on if, for example, you had to climb a mountain and needed a companion, had a girl lamb that lost her ear tag in the brambles and so became known as Notag, which had a nice Welsh ring to it. Jenny raised all three of her lambs — two boys and a girl — although any experienced shepherd will tell you that puts a tremendous strain on a Romney ewe.

My first impression not withstanding, raising sheep was one of the greatest challenges of my life (even more difficult than assembling a gas barbecue). I was picking up information from a variety of sources — over-the-back-fence chats with Chuck and Angela, Jan the farmer who'd sold us three of the Gang of Five and books that told me more than I hoped to remember. Unlike chickens, which tend to be either healthy or dead, the sheep had more subtle health problems that I, inexperienced as I was, failed to spot.

For instance, Jenny's triplets were weaned too late and, as we weren't properly set up to separate mums from lambs, and I was busy and distracted by all the other new farm tasks, Jenny paid the price. At three months of age the boys were so big that they had to kneel, one on each side, to get the upward angle of their mouths on each teat. When they were feeding they pushed so hard they nearly lifted her back legs off the ground. When they finally backed off, the girl would have her turn. Recalling her own experience as a new mother, Christine said, "Ouch."

One day I noticed Jenny wasn't out in the field with the others. I found her with her threesome, standing in the shade of the barn roof, head into the corner, ears down. If one of her lambs attempted to feed from her she'd kick at it half-heartedly and limp off, obviously in pain. When I approached her she didn't run away — unusual. Her udder looked swollen and red and was very hot to the touch. She had mastitis, a serious illness in a sheep as the inflamed tissue never recovers; she would never be able to feed lambs again. This would mean bottle-feeding, sleepless nights and lambs with health problems. I should cull her before the next breeding season, but she wasn't just any ewe, she was Jenny. She had been named.

Her lambs were forced out with the others and summarily weaned, while Jenny stayed in the barn and endured, over the next several days, my inexpert jabs with a needle full of antibiotics to bring down her fever. Amazingly she survived, though perhaps damaged psychologically by my ineptness and certainly physically by the mastitis. But as spring turned into summer I put her medical condition out of mind as best I could and turned my attention to the other tasks on the farm.

Autumn arrived and the ewes were in heat, staring through the fence at Eric. And I, in a fit of udder stupidity and laziness, left Jenny with the flock on the day when I opened the gate and allowed them to mingle. She became pregnant. Once again I avoided contemplating her condition even as the winter eased toward March and lambing time. She likely would not have any milk, and especially none of the mother's first milk (the colostrum, full of the nutrition and antibodies newborns need. The previous year I had managed to milk a little colostrum from one of the other sheep and had it stored in the freezer for just such an emergency. It wasn't much, so if Jenny were the first to lamb we were probably in deep trouble. If, however, the other ewes lambed ahead of her, I might be able to milk extra colostrum from them *after* their lambs had fed and use it to get Jenny's lambs through their crucial first few days.

The winter crept along, the ewes fattening and "bagging out," their bellies distending and dropping as the lambs grew. On a cold night in early March, two days after Norah had produced a pair of twins that had taken most of her milk, Jenny lay down in the straw and effortlessly delivered a boy and girl. She was quickly up on her feet, cleaning them, while they wobbled, crying (a sound uncannily human) for their first feeding. Anxious and hunched against the cold, I watched silently from outside the pen. In short order the lambs found the teats, but even a rank amateur like me could see they weren't getting fed. I ran back up to the house, got the colostrum, thawed it and mixed it with some heated, freshly purchased goats' milk in a beer bottle, stretched the nipple over the end, then returned to the barn, prepared to be a wet-nurse once more.

Both lambs took to the bottle with gusto, so after they had drunk their fill I moved them and their mother into one of the small pens where ewes and newborns spent their first 48 hours. Turning off the lights, I went back to the house to thaw myself out and sleep. About four hours later, at dawn, I shook myself awake and trudged back down to the barn, where the two bright-eyed lambs and their rather perplexed mother awaited me. The lambs had already figured out that I was the source of the food, while the big white object in the pen with them kept them warm and gave them an occasional lick. They seemed fine and their care and maintenance looked like a challenge I could cope with, much as I would with sleep deprivation.

It was all too good to be true, of course. Although the boy continued to do well, the girl picked up an infection. She ran a temperature, became listless, rejected the bottle and soon resembled a mere woolly rag compared with her robust brother. I tried all the tonics and supplements in the book, but nothing seemed to reverse her decline. Each morning I'd lift her out of the straw onto the warmth of my lap. She stirred, but when I tried to feed her with a plastic syringe the milk just dribbled out of the side of her mouth. Her gums turned pale and her eyes dull.

Jenny had already ceased to pay attention to the lamb and watched me quietly while I fussed about. She adopted an admonishing look that asked, "Why do you try to keep those that want to die, alive?" Her pragmatic attitude reminded me of a friend whose family had a history of heart problems; he had DO NOT RESUSCITATE tattooed over his left breast (it took him a while to get around to it, not because he was having second thoughts, but because he couldn't make up his mind about the typeface).

After a few more Florence Nightingale days and nights, I regained my common sense. Instead of continuing to maintain a vigil, one morning when the lamb was barely breathing I left her in the straw. Jenny and her bottle baby had already graduated from the confines of the lambing pen and rejoined the flock out in the field.

I had to tell myself to let the invalid be. Christine and I put on our hiking boots and went for a walk in the nearby park, listening to the birds as they courted and sang while building their nests. New lives, springtime, the natural order of things.

On the way home, we were nearly at our gate when Bill hailed us from his field. He had been clearing fallen branches from the woods at the back of his property and hauling them to a burning pile with the help of his two draught horses. Bill had been a teacher who ranched, or a rancher who taught school, and had once raised cattle in the north, where you don't have the backup of vets and local slaughterhouses to help you out. He had probably seen it all in his time. I told him about Jenny, my stupidity in breeding her and the little rag of a lamb dying in the straw. I felt so guilty, so *responsible*.

"Yeah, you gotta cull the runts, that's for sure," he drawled.

I muttered something about how lazy I'd been.

"Reminds me of a cow I had once, called Lucky," he said. "We were living up in the Peace Country and I was teaching school. One day, my wife was checking the cattle and thought one was having some trouble, so she called me at the school and told me I should come home straight away, but she didn't say why."

He shifted his weight and put a boot up on the fence rail: "I didn't think it was urgent so I ran a couple of errands in town on the way and by the time I got home she was mad. She'd been out to check the cow again and it was obviously in trouble. So I grabbed my calf chains and off we went into the snow to find the cow and pull the calf. I figured it'd probably be dead, but at least we'd save the cow."

A smile broke on his face. "Well, the calf was all twisted up inside her, but we got it out alive! Sort of. The cow took one look at it and moved off. I guess the umbilical cord had been pinched, so it had brain damage.

"There was nothin' to do but take the calf into the house and raise it, so I threw it over my shoulder and carried it home. And you know, we raised that calf in the kitchen...named her Lucky."

"Did she get over the brain damage?" I asked.

"Naw, not really, but she went out with the other calves and figured out how to eat grass and — just like you — I got busy with other things and didn't send her to market. The next thing I knew she was pregnant.

"I just couldn't kill a pregnant cow. So Lucky went through her term and gave birth to a calf smarter than his mother. He led her around all over the place. But I couldn't let it happen twice, so as soon as the calf was weaned I had to deal with Lucky."

"You shipped her to market?"

"Well, as it turned out, no. You see, I figured that because she was a pet, the kindest thing I could do was to kill her at home. Less stressful for her. My daughter's never eaten beef since."

We whiled away a few more minutes in chat about the weather and local politics before walking the last few paces home. I went directly to the barn where the lamb lay, unmoved in her nest of clean straw. The weather was still too cold for flies. Her sides moved ever so slightly. Don't touch her, I told myself. Leave her be.

The following morning she was dead. Christine buried her in the garden and planted a rosebush over her; her remains attracted bugs and maggots that attracted a mole that tunnelled under and around the rose. But that's farming for you.

Easter was late that year and in our valley it was springtime at its most verdant: green leaves and fields, dandelions dotting the meadows, cumulus clouds in the breezy sky and...Greeks roaming the country roads looking for lambs for their Easter dinner.

Richard and Maureen, acquaintances who also raised sheep, had explained this springtime ritual. Greeks like a small lamb of about 50 to 60 pounds that will dress out to 25 or 30, perfect for roasting whole for a family feast. My first reaction was positive until Richard and Maureen went on to say they had stopped selling at their farmgate after one group slaughtered the lamb on the public road beside their mailbox. I asked a few sheep-owning neighbours what they did and received a predictable range of responses.

"They pay top price!" said the old farmers.

"The lambs are so little, and the men are such amateur butchers! Won't have anything to do with it!" said the urban refugees.

It never occurred to me that I'd have to deal with this, as our farm was on a dead-end road. However, one Saturday morning, when I was in the barn and Christine was in her garden, I heard a horn.

"There's a car at the gate," she called to me. "It's probably JWs — you deal with them!"

As we weren't as intolerant as some of our neighbours who had signs on their gates with the letters *JW* in a circle with a diagonal slash through it, we got the occasional carload of Jehovah's Witnesses. The ones most certain of their faith would enter any property and, carrying their Bibles and pamphlets, march through packs of slavering Rottweilers to the farmhouse.

Today's callers were evidently more circumspect.

Firm politeness being the best policy, I strode toward the gate, but was surprised to see a Mercedes sedan, not the sort of four-door with blackwall tires I was expecting. Three men emerged, all casually dressed, none of them sporting the sober suit and short-back-and-sides of the typical JW scouting party.

"Got any lambs for sale?" one asked, a gold filling in a front tooth catching the sun.

Completely unprepared for this turn of events, I began to mumble.

"Ah, er, umm ... lemme see, well ... ahhh. I don't think any of them are big enough and...ahhh...*no*."

"We need one for Easter dinner tomorrow — we've tried everywhere, no one will sell to us," a second one pleaded.

Being open-minded and generally in favour of supporting ethnic customs in an era of globalization, I wavered a little, but couldn't see what else I could do. If I pulled a lamb away from its mother, I'd have to dry the mother out very quickly or she'd be in danger of getting mastitis, just like...Jenny. Jenny's boy! I was going to have to cull him anyway and he was costing me a fortune in goats' milk.

"Well, maybe I've got one, but he might be a little small."

Rather grimly, as in a nightmare, I went out into the field and clapped my hands. All the sheep looked up and Jenny's boy bounded eagerly toward me. I grabbed him and carried him back to the men, who gathered round, nodded, checked his hind legs for meat quantity and talked excitedly in Greek.

"Okay, we'll take him. How much, please?"

"Fifty bucks, but you can't kill him here!" I answered rather desperately. I had spent at least that amount on milk and, after all, I was trying to be practical.

"Okay, okay, we'll take him home."

We trussed up the lamb with binder twine and put him on a piece of cardboard in the trunk. As the Mercedes pulled away, I went into the garden to find Christine.

"Now I feel like a *real* farmer," I pronounced glumly.

Jenny bawled for two days (as all sheep do when their lambs are weaned). I, too, was depressed. However, I began to realize that the problem was not the livestock themselves, but my lack of management, lack of control. In the city, I had rarely imposed my will on any creature and, like most people, allowed the kitty to stay inside on a rainy night even though I *knew* he would wake me up at three o'clock in the morning. Jan had divined this softness in my character when I'd told him how the sheep always wanted to go into the wrong field. He advised with an amused twinkle in his eye, "Remember — they're the sheep and you're the shepherd."

Accordingly, I culled Jenny. She now holds a job as a lawn mower at a place nearby owned by people only interested in having a big woolly pet. For all I know, she's alive today.

The Arthurian Legend

We chose our first rooster almost at random, at dawn on an October morning. About five months earlier I had bought two dozen day-old Barred Rock chicks, "open run" as the hatcheries describe them — that is, unsorted by sex. We thought we would raise a dozen or so hens, pick a cockerel to become our rooster and turn the unlucky ones into *coq au vin*. The only criterion we used in our selection was to pick one who would bump off our particularly aggressive cockerel, an avian Mike Tyson, that had earned his spurs by repeatedly beating up his brothers. He would, in time, we were sure, make our lives miserable too.

As it turned out, the one we picked took charge so we named him Arthur. King Arthur. As befitted his role, he grew into a large creature with beautiful plumage, "barred" or striped in black and white, with a magnificent cape of stiff hackles at his neck and a marvellous fountain of black-and-white tail feathers. His comb and wattles were the brightest crimson and his yellow legs were complemented by a yellow rim around his bright, beady eyes. By the time he was a year old his spurs had grown to more than two inches, curved upward and viciously sharp. Every fall, when he moulted, I gathered up his old tail feathers and glued them to the feather duster. He was a classic male — preening and pompous, the embodiment of the word "cocksure." Why have a rooster? To make more chickens, mainly, although we had also read that roosters kept order in the henhouse and were the cheapest form of home entertainment.

A day in the life of Arthur: crow at dawn, peck a little grain, strut about the barnyard, casually mount passing hens, fly up onto a gate or ascend a manure pile every once in a while to survey the kingdom, warn the hens (who were always head-down and pecking for food) of passing hawks and eagles and crow whenever one of the neighbour's roosters started up.

"Oh, listen," our friend Sharon said one day when Arthur began to sound off in response to the distant crowing of another rooster, "they're saying 'hello' to each other!"

"More like 'get lost' than 'hello,'" I replied. "They're defining their turf." At the time, Sharon owned only horses and dogs.

A day in the life of a hen: get woken at dawn by the deafening reveille of the lord and master a few feet away from your ear; peck grain; wander about, neck in the fore-and-back sway of poultry in motion; when nature calls, head for a favourite nest, preferably a dark, out-of-the-way place, to lay an egg that your owner won't find, but make such a *pok-pok-pok-pok* racket that it defeats your secretive intentions; have a dust bath in a convenient spot; head back to the roost at dusk; go to sleep crooning songs from the chicken hit parade.

Arthur ran the barnyard and took no nonsense from any other poultry, including the much-larger gander, Jethro. Occasionally he became too aggressive and would hang around behind me, waiting for the appropriate moment to leap at my calves and gore me with his spurs, but I soon came to recognize his black moods and stuck a boot in his face to keep him back. More often he was calm and in control, adored by his hens and our city friends, who insisted on paying him a visit when they dropped by. He even got a few Christmas cards.

Arthur was the only one with a name. After all, he was distinctive and flamboyant, while the hens were pretty tough to tell apart. Like modest Victorian wives, they were neat and tidy, their small red wattles and combs like tied-down bonnets, their black-and-white feathers tight to their bodies. It helped that they were nameless, as occasionally one would be invited to dinner with us or would be convicted of the offence of egg-eating, which was really the only capital crime in the henhouse. To be honest, we weren't interested in eating our hens, as once they were past six months of age they lost a certain *je ne sais quoi* in the taste department and had to be boiled almost to rags to make them tender enough for our weak, modern teeth. Instead we counted on the hens to "go broody" — to sit and hatch eggs — and provide us with a self-sustaining flock, including cockerels to go into the cooking pot once they grew to the size usually sold in supermarkets as "fryers."

All in all, the Barred Rocks were a very satisfactory breed and I crowed inwardly when Jan, the farmer who had started us on sheep, took a liking to our chickens and decided to raise a dozen of his own. Unlike us, however, he kept the meanest of his half dozen cockerels, a hulking brute who attacked anyone entering his domain. Jan's grandchildren became terrified of the rooster, refused to go anywhere near the henhouse and showed less and less interest in coming out to the farm for Sunday dinner, preferring instead to stay home and watch the latest news from the Balkans.

Coincidentally, *our* hens had hatched cockerels who were wandering around the barnyard, keeping out of Arthur's way as best they could. Although we had done our utmost to keep their prospects a secret from them, one of them obviously had read the script in advance and developed a survival strategy that involved flying over the fence and helping Christine in the flower garden. He became adept at following her around, pecking at the occasional weed and beaking up any bugs or worms she came upon while weeding — an environmentally friendly pesticide. It all went according to his plan, for Christine became quite fond of him and refused to allow me to chop his head off when he became big enough that Arthur, too, wanted to kill him. But Arthur had spoken: "This barn-yard isn't big enough for the two of us," so the hunt was on for a new home for Christine's pet.

Jan had given his rooster to a shepherd named Martin, whose own rooster had dropped dead suddenly in the pasture behind his house. Martin's property backed onto a subdivision, where people evidently preferred the noise of stereos, leaf-blowers and Harley-Davidsons to the dawn chorus of roosters. According to Jan there had been words across the back fence and the next thing Martin knew his rooster was dead. As there were no gunshot wounds, or pieces of steak dripping with strychnine, Martin chugged off to the local agricultural office to get an autopsy done on the carcass and learned, to his relief, that the bird had expired from a heart attack — an occupational hazard for any creature that fornicates a dozen or more times a day. Hearing this tale, Jan offered Martin *his* rooster, but that didn't last long as the malevolent creature savagely attacked Martin's daughter, who promptly went on strike and refused to do any chores around the henhouse.

Jan regaled us with this story one day over coffee. All joking aside, he said he now needed a rooster, as his hens were beginning to squabble and feather-pick each other in their quarters. That's the problem with having just a *hen*house — the hens establish a rigid pecking order and spend so much time working on it, like children in a schoolyard, that they have little energy left to do anything useful. A rooster's job is to make sure all hens are equal.

Christine's pet, appropriately named Lucky (though not after Bill's mentally challenged cow), went off to Jan's, where he retained his pleasant temperament while overseeing a half dozen hens. Once again, Jan's grandchildren could be sent off to gather the eggs without fear.

From time to time we added chickens to the flock, experimenting with other old breeds like Rhode Island Reds, but their personalities were less pleasant. Although we weren't actually seeking to befriend them, we wanted them to be comfortable with themselves and easygoing, not constantly agitated, flighty, itinerant or otherwise unmanageable.

Our Rhode Island Reds wandered and explored, more Eric the Red than Rhode Island Red. Sometimes we'd see a hen far off in the field, exposed to any hawk that happened to be flying by, oblivious to how far she had ranged. We checked the henhouse for a suicide note and got out the binoculars to make sure she wasn't carrying a suitcase. Free-range is one thing, but this .... They were putting too much energy into hiking and not nearly enough into egg-making. I was so uninterested in eating their well-exercised, sinewy bodies that I took them to the auction, where they sold for $6 each.

Eventually even some of the Barred Rock hens began to annoy us. They were a bit too adventurous and were constantly challenging the fences separating the barnyard from the flower and vegetable gardens. A rooster will go exploring just to conquer new territory, and although occasionally he will spear a bug or clip a tasty blade of grass on his way through, he does little damage. A typical rooster grazes like a well-fed human at a cocktail party. But a hen is different: needing huge quantities of plants and bugs in order to keep producing eggs, she forages systematically. Needless to say, this is disaster for garden seedlings. Five minutes of scratching by a single hen can demolish a whole row of lettuce. On the other hand, hens are useful in the fall, scratching up and eating overwintering bugs that would likely rampage the following year.

Although we had good gates and wire fences, they all had a

top railing, which the chickens could see and reach. Chickens, dogs and coyotes don't jump *over* barriers — they jump *to* them and then spring off onto the other side — so you can fool a chicken with a low fence that has just wire at the top. You also can clip their wings to ground them, but that makes them even more vulnerable to predators. As a teenager growing up in the city it had never occurred to me that clipping wings and grounding were terms applied elsewhere.

The Barred Rocks' flighty habits made me realize I was not the laid-back, *laissez-faire*, do-as-you-please sort of person I had always believed myself to be. Although I had managed to stay cool even during the frenetic 1980s, and had raised a daughter with only the occasional threat to send her to a convent, the act of farming had revealed my true personality: I was a control freak.

Beyond the management of these free spirits, there was the matter of dinner. We were always short of chickens for the pot. Although I could easily have chugged out to the local hatchery whenever I wanted chicks, and raised them under a heat lamp as I had with Arthur and his flock, I had a romantic view of farm-ing in which, as in a storybook, the farmers live in a self-contained world. Putting aside the problems created by inbreeding the livestock, I wanted a sustainable farm that would survive stock-market meltdowns, Y2K crises and the environ-mental wreckage caused by factory farms. Happy animals, a bucolic lifestyle — that's what I was after, so, dammit, these animals had to be prolific or else they were soup!

In theory, of course, a chicken is smart enough to be a chicken and that is all she need be. However, the modern chicken is certainly an underachiever compared with the great chickens of yore. Yes, she can manufacture eggs, but it is a rare hen that has the smarts necessary to *sit* eggs and hatch chicks. As the seasons went by, we became increasingly frustrated by the Barred Rock hens who, in terms of mothering abilities, were a few sandwiches short of a picnic. Example: you go into the henhouse late in the afternoon to gather the eggs and there is a hen in one of the nesting boxes, puffed up and self-important atop a clutch of eggs. You put a hand in to touch her back and she flares out all her feathers and lets out a low squeal, fierce and reptilian. She whips her beak around to peck at your hand, but makes no move to flee. Ergo, she's a broody. The next morning, you go back to let the chickens out and check on her and find she's still on her eggs, lost in her thoughts. However, when you go down later in the day she's moved to another nest! What happened? She got off to look for food and water, which is natural (and is nature's way of allowing the eggs to cool down), but when she returned she got confused and hopped up into another nest that had fresh eggs in it! Alternatively, partway through the 21-day incubation period she might lose interest in sitting and abandon the eggs, wasting them. (According to our vintage cookbooks, eggs can be used for cooking until they've been brooded for nine days. We were unwilling to try the old farming delicacy of an embryo further developed.)

If I left a broody hen in a normal nesting box, other hens would sometimes jump in with her to lay their eggs, which would then be scooped under the broody. As these were on a different cycle from the eggs she was already sitting, they'd be wasted when she got off the nest after her chicks hatched. Although I looked through the self-help hobby-farmer chicken books at the co-op and browsed the myriad chicken sites on the Internet, seeking advice, I could find nothing. Maybe everybody else had chickens smarter than ours? Regardless, I had to take charge.

The broodies needed to be confined to a crèche, so I jerry-rigged a wire enclosure at one end of the henhouse. It was an improvement in chicken management if not in construction and, subject to the limitations of our chickens' refusal to take motherhood seriously, we were making progress. In the crèche, the only misbehaviour was an occasional bout of egg-stealing that I had to referee. At feeding time I took to humming the Dire Straits song about getting your chicks for free.

As a fallback position, I bought at a garage sale a small incubator that looked like the plastic foam used to pack my last stereo. The man having the sale looked gaunt and haggard, selling his farm equipment before moving to a place where all the food came in cans. Not surprisingly, results, using the incubator, were rather inconsistent, with a success rate of about 50 percent. To make matters worse, some of the chicks seemed slightly mentally retarded — although, to be honest, it was tough to tell — probably because the temperature was too high or the humidity too low. Nevertheless, I wasn't prepared to spend $800 or $1,000 for a really good incubator in order to hatch $100 worth of chicks a year.

One day our friends Karen and Keith came for tea and were admiring the chickens wandering around in the barnyard. Keith had a city job and was off to catch the train each morning before even the roosters got up, leaving Karen to manage a hobby farm not unlike ours, with a handful of sheep and a huge vegetable garden. The sheep were the relics of a yardful of critters they had acquired and nurtured when they first moved from the city several years earlier. Unlike ours, though, their fields bordered a forest that was home to marauding packs of coyotes and chicken-chomping, cat-maiming raccoons and weasels. Sometimes at night, when we (as visitors) looked across their pasture to the forest, we could almost see the twin beams of coyote eyes looking back; they were customers at a rural drive-in restaurant. All the couple's poultry, purchased as pets, had been scarfed down. Their children had grown up and moved on, no doubt psychologically scarred by seeing

partially eaten bodies strewn around the yard. Keith and Karen
had never replaced their chickens and, lacking the will to be
in control (like me), they had grudgingly come to accept the loss
of the occasional ewe or lamb.

The antics of our chickens prompted Karen to recount
stories of her childhood on a farm in Alberta. Her father had
been a teacher in a country school who farmed haphazardly in
his spare time. Her mother, since widowed but once a classic
farm wife, had become so determined not to be tied down by
anything that she refused to own even a houseplant. Karen had
memories of the turkeys her father used to raise, especially a
nasty gobbler that had harassed her. It also once attacked her
mother, who picked up a stick and hit it on the head, causing
one of its eyes to pop out and dangle by the optic nerve until
a neighbour was summoned to push it back into its socket. We
made a mental note not to raise turkeys.

Karen had fonder memories of her childhood chickens: Buff
Orpingtons, a placid, old-fashioned English variety (from
Orpington in Kent), one of the best of the "dual-purpose"
breeds — chickens that laid enough eggs over the course of a
year to justify what you fed them, but were meaty enough to
make a meal. Responding to our complaints about the difficulty
in keeping some of the Barred Rocks on the correct side of any
fence, Karen commented, "My Buffs were always head-down and
scratching. The ground was their world. They were sitting
ducks, if that's the right term, for hawks."

"Remember your mom's rooster, Karen?" Keith asked,
grinning. "Nothing happened without him noticing — he'd
call the hens together as soon as he spotted a hawk."

"Keith thought our old rooster was *such* a hero," Karen
laughed. "He died of his wounds after attacking a fox that had
grabbed one of the hens."

"He was such a *romantic* character. I think the hen survived," said Keith. He loved the chivalrous, almost-medieval world of poultry in a barnyard.

"I've never seen Buffs advertised," Karen added. "I guess they've just died out as a breed around here."

"There were a few at the show last fall," I said, referring to the annual poultry-fancier's exhibition at the Fall Fair nearby. Christine and I had attended out of curiosity, but retreated from the spectacle of exotic, pampered, groomed birds in cages, mainly roosters. Their obsessive owners shuffled around and fussed. It was all a bit much.

"I doubt they'd be much good as farm chickens," said Karen. "Too much inbreeding, not enough natural behaviour. My old Buffs were great mothers."

There were, in fact, only two classic chicken breeds available from the local hatchery: Barred Rocks and the roamin' Reds. The only other chicks you could buy were modern hybrids, either specialized egg-layers (the source of the standard supermarket egg, either white or brown), or Cornish Giants (the mainstay of the boneless-chicken-breast industry). Although we raised a couple of dozen Cornish Giants as roasting chickens each summer, the specialized egg-layers didn't interest us. Like anything hybrid (including the vegetable seeds that are the mainstay of agribusiness), they don't breed true, and the second generation of hybridization is usually a weakling.

"If I could get Buffs, I'd get back into chickens," Karen said as they were getting into the car.

"If *I* could get Buffs," I replied, "I wouldn't have to spend so much time chasing chickens out of the garden and there'd be more to eat."

From time to time I scanned the local papers for ads offering SMALL FLOCK OF BUFFS FOR SALE CHEAP. Then one day a city friend handed Christine a catalogue with, on its cover, a bright, *art naif* painting of a chicken held in the arms of a freckle-faced girl with braids and bangs and a checked gingham dress. It was from Murray McMurray Hatchery in Webster City, Iowa, in business since 1917. Christine flipped through page after page of exotic chickens: multicoloured bantams, rare Polish and Houdan chickens with crests like turbans, Cochin chickens with feathered feet, pheasants, geese, ducks, turkeys, guinea hens and partridges. You could even get a peacock! Like zoos for wild animals in an era of species extinction, this hatchery was a Noah's Ark in an era of factory farms. On page 12, in the "Heavy Breeds" section, were Buff Orpingtons.

"Introduced from England in the late 1800s, they became one of the most popular farm fowls in this country," the catalogue stated. Scanning the paragraph, I read "stately, quiet, beautiful eating, excellent setters and mothers" — my dream chicken. At U.S. $1.47 each. I flipped to the back to read about shipping and handling.

I phoned Karen. "I can get Buffs!"

"Get a dozen for me!" she said with excitement.

Although we had never ordered chickens by mail before, we understood the principle: a chick is hatched with enough energy to enable it to survive for about two days before it needs food or water. Watching our broody hens, we realized that if they got off the nest immediately to find food for their first chick, then each hen would hatch only a single chick. Instead, the hen's internal clock keeps her sitting on the eggs and chicks for 48 hours, at which time she abandons any remaining eggs and sallies forth, her chicks in tow, to look for food and water. On such natural rhythms the poultry-by-post industry was born: motherless chicks from incubators are packed in boxes and whisked off across the land.

Although Iowa is in the United States and, the last time we looked, we were in Canada, the catalogue suggested that cross-border chick shipments were no problem. I picked up the phone and dialed Murray McMurray's toll-free number.

"How may ah help you?" asked the sweet, Midwestern-accented voice on the other end of the line.

I explained our situation and was told that, for a fee of $12, a health certificate and hatching papers suitable for customs clearance would be prepared and shipped with the chicks by UPS to General Delivery at the post office in Lynden, Washington, just on the other side of the border.

"Our friends in Canada have no trouble with customs, ah can assure you," said the voice on the phone.

Two dozen was the minimum number they shipped, so I chose the open-run option, just as I had with the Arthur gang a few years earlier. We settled on a delivery date in early March, she took my credit card number, we thanked each other effusively. Before she hung up, she assured me that the post office would call me when the chicks arrived. Wonderful people, those Americans — so *organized*.

The night before the appointed date, I set up my portable, all-purpose chicken cage — a bottomless box of lath and chicken wire lashed together — hung an infrared light inside and filled a couple of drip trays (the kind you put under a small plant pot) with water. Chicks that are motherless start eating feed scattered on a piece of newspaper. I always try to use the art reviews from a national newspaper to give them a good start, before moving them onto bedding of chopped straw or wood shavings. Without a mother hen to show them what's edible, they're likely to waste time pecking up the bedding, so I keep it as simple as possible.

As we lacked the regimentation of cow-milking or commuting to a job, we often made a slow start in the morning, and we were sitting over coffee at 8:02 a.m. when the phone rang. When I picked it up I could hear a shrill noise in the background. A bad connection?

Over the din a voice said, "Lynden post office here. Got some chicks for you — *how soon can you come pick 'em up?*"

The voice sounded a little strangled, but suddenly I understood: the accompanying noise was the sound of chicks peeping in unison. It's a sound that penetrates your thoughts like a smoke alarm piercing a sweet dream.

"Half an hour," I replied, reaching for my coat.

In mere minutes, after thundering over the country roads, I arrived beneath the fluttering Stars and Stripes on the main street of Lynden.

With the front door open only a crack I could hear the chicks. A few customers scuttled by quickly, clutching their social security cheques and NRA newsletters. The postal workers were clustered in one corner of the room. Hesitantly I approached the counter. "I'm here to pick up...."

"Sign here!" urged a woman with a pained expression on her face as she pushed a form at me. Another employee rushed over to a shelf and pulled down a carton, about the size of a small shoebox, from which all the racket was emanating. If it had been a stereo speaker it would have been a tweeter.

"You have a good day now!" the postal workers chorused.

I lifted a corner of the lid and there, packed in, were 24 fluffy blond critters, with yellow beaks and bright eyes, looking up expectantly. They were hungry and thirsty, maybe even cold and doubtless footsore after being packed together wing to wing for at least 36 hours. I hightailed it back to the border.

"How long you been down?" the Canadian customs officer asked from his booth.

"About 20 minutes — just went to the post office to pick up some chicks."

"Got papers?"

"Yup."

"Bring 'em in."

I parked and carried my precious cargo inside. A serious young woman, in a crisp blue shirt and tie and her official WE STAND ON GUARD FOR THEE customs cap, was behind the counter. I put down the cheeping carton and handed her the envelope containing what I presumed were the health papers. She ran her practised eye over the fine print, reached into a drawer for a stamp and whacked it on the appropriate forms; one copy went into a basket on the counter and she handed the other back to me. So far so good.

"I just have to inspect them," she said in her professional tone, lifting the lid on the box. The din intensified. Picking up the box, she headed toward a room at the back. "I'll be right back," she said over her shoulder as she retreated. What did an inspection involve? Scientists wearing lab coats? Pincers and thermometers?

Not quite. Suddenly there was a chorus of, "Aww, how sweet!" and "Ooh, cute!" When she reappeared she was smiling. As she handed the box back, she said, "We don't get many animals anymore. Too bad." She shrugged.

Fifteen minutes later I was home and the chicks were eating and drinking and scratching around under the heat lamp.

>─┼─◆>─○─<◆─┼─<

Over the next few weeks the clutch of chicks feathered out and grew. Karen and Keith had built a predator-proof chicken stockade at their place and, once the chicks were into their fourth week and could be weaned from the electric light, Karen came over and picked up half of them. Ours moved over into the run with the meat chickens and as summer progressed they grew large and beautiful on their diet of grain, weeds, bugs and anything we discovered at the back of the fridge. We took to bringing home doggy bags from restaurants. It was all

Christine could do to stop me from asking other diners if they *really* wanted to finish everything on their plates.

By autumn the Buff pullets were ready to join the main gang in the henhouse. While Arthur was naturally delighted to welcome the new girls into the flock, the old Barred Rock hens were initially quite aggressive, pecking and chasing them. I came to realize that the word *placid* in the catalogue was a synonym for *dumb*.

Meanwhile, we still had to select a rooster so we could raise purebred Buff chicks the following year. But which to choose? There was no identifiable bruiser to cull from our half dozen cockerels, as with Arthur's brothers. However, there was a variation in colour among them, so I selected one that had particularly beautiful, rich gold feathers tinged with orange — the colour of an old-fashioned pocket watch, the hallmark of a classic Buff Orpington. The other cockerels ended up in the freezer, their feathers incorporated into the duster. The survivor, who seemed a little stunned but quite good-natured, was named Dave after a scarcely competent tradesman we had once employed.

Like a convict "inside" for too long, Dave joined the larger community and tried to fit in. For the first few days Arthur didn't seem to notice him. Dave bumbled around on the outskirts of the flock, keeping his beak shut. Eventually, though, he began to attract attention to himself by doing what a rooster's gotta do. The old hens would have none of it, faithful as they were to Arthur. They ran as fast as they could, with Dave in hot pursuit, the smart ones heading for Arthur. Dave was often so intent on his chase that he would practically crash into Arthur before he realized what he was doing.

At other times Dave would manage to seize a hen by the neck, but as he was still a bit small and rather uncoordinated, he would lose his balance while attempting to swing himself into position atop the hen. Arthur, after years of practice, had developed a very deft technique, to the point that a hen, hearing his rapid footfall, usually just lay down, waited, and thought of England. By comparison Dave was comical, flapping his wings to keep from tumbling backward, unable to pull the pinned hen's neck back to the right angle or to lower his centre of gravity by dropping his wings to the ground beside her. The Buff hens' only experience had been with Dave's clumsy teenage brothers, so they, too, gravitated to Arthur. Even harder on Dave's self-esteem, in mid-grapple he would sometimes be set upon by a couple of other hens and knocked off by a sharp peck or two to the side of his head. *Coitus interruptus.*

Poor Dave. He would shuffle off to crow by himself, far away from Arthur. Arthur would respond, loud and triumphant, confident of his control of the barnyard. In the evening both roosters went back to the henhouse, but Arthur always went in first, selecting a spot on a favourite rafter where he had an unimpeded view of the doorway. A couple of his pet hens usually took positions on either side of him. Then, as the last light faded from the sky, Dave would skulk in and find a spot on the perch, but as far away as possible. He learned to wait until Arthur had gone out with the hens in the morning. At feeding time, I would call him over, out of sight of the others, to give him some grain, so he became almost tame. He was forced to move home and live in the shadow of his overbearing stepfather. Not knowing what use he'd be, we considered taking out a life-insurance policy and entering him in a cockfight.

Spring arrived; time to separate the chickens so that the eggs we incubated would give us only purebred chicks. One night I went down to the henhouse, lifted Dave and his half dozen snoozing Buff hens off the perch two-by-two and carried them over to the vacant meat-chicken compound (which needed a new name: Daveburg? Daveville?). Here Dave, for the first time, could have his own home and harem and once and for all be boss.

Almost immediately there was a change in his personality. He stood taller and could soon be found with a clutch of hens around him. He crowed often, with a much clearer, louder sound than before, inciting Arthur to start up elsewhere in the barnyard. I began to gather eggs for the incubator, both from Daveburg and from the main henhouse, and found after a week that a couple of the Buff hens had gone broody. All was going well.

Three weeks later the incubator had hatched about 20 chicks, some pale blond, the Barred Rocks almost black. The brood-ies had produced a few chicks each and were fussing with them, scratching through the dirt for bugs and seeds that they placed on the ground with an expression that declaimed, "Try this!" I collected a final batch of eggs from the two sets of chickens and then, to make Daveburg available for the growing chicks from the incubator and the arrival of the meat chickens, I moved Dave and the Buffs back into the henhouse with Arthur and the Barred Rock hens. Dave was now easily Arthur's size; at worst they'd have a shoving match. Or so I thought.

It wasn't the first day they were together, but perhaps the second or the third, that there was a terrible fight. I missed the first round, but Dave had obviously looked the wrong way at Arthur and had paid an awful price. Although Arthur was undamaged, Dave was drenched in blood. Arthur had practi-cally torn his comb off. By morning the blond feathers on his head had dried into a bloody helmet; he had reverted to his submissive, shuffling self and he kept out of Arthur's way. They never fought again.

I, too, had learned a lesson. The following year I kept Dave and his Buffs apart from the others for only four or five days at a stretch, long enough to ensure that the eggs I was collecting for the incubator were purebred. Two or three times that spring, under the stars, with the sheep looking quizzically at me, I'd hike back and forth between Daveburg and the henhouse, a chicken under each arm.

>─┼─◆>─·O─·<◆─┼─<

The spring that Arthur turned four he developed a curious habit: he would fly up onto the gate that separated the barnyard from the flower garden, crow briefly, then leap down onto the lawn and begin to eat dandelion flowers. Great habit, we agreed, having no inclination to weed the grass ourselves. As dandelions are a classic potherb renowned for their medicinal qualities (in fact their Latin name, *Taraxacum officinale*, means "the cure for disorders"), we wondered whether Arthur sought an essential vitamin or narcotic he needed to maintain his lifestyle. An avian Viagra, perhaps. Nobody of our acquaintance had ever heard of a rooster doing this before and the University of Texas chicken website made no reference to such bizarre behaviour. Chicken lore is getting a bit hard to find in these modern times. As the dandelions faded, Arthur ceased to fly over into the garden, which pleased us: he was a bad role model for his adventurous Barred Rock hens.

The following spring, as millions of dandelions came into flower, Arthur again began to fly into the garden. But this time he seemed obsessed, spending much of the day on his own, walking slowly from flower to flower, sometimes tasting the yellow petals, at other times biting off and swallowing the entire thing. Periodically, he'd stand very still, his head on his chest and his tail feathers pointing downward, looking for all the world as if he was trying to impersonate a Great Blue Heron. "Arthur's stoned again," we'd say to each other.

Earlier that season he had briefly lost the top note of his crow and sounded rather gutteral, like an over-the-hill opera tenor who was only able to hit high B. I wondered if he had picked up a minor respiratory infection, but as the weather cleared and warmed in March and April he recovered.

Over the next couple of weeks, however, he became more and more quiet. After a brief flurry of activity in the morning, pecking at grain, he would stand silently near a spruce tree in the corner of the barnyard where many of the hens groomed themselves in the midday sun. I went down to the henhouse one night with the flashlight and found him in his familiar spot on the perch, checked him over for wounds and signs of disease, but found nothing. When I lifted him off the perch to have a closer look I realized he didn't weigh much more than a bag of feathers — he was obviously having trouble processing food and was slowly starving to death.

I began to check him every night and soon discovered he was no longer able to fly up onto the perch. He was spending the night in a nesting box near the floor, where he lay quietly on top of a few eggs. A day or two later he became as immobile as a lawn statue. I picked him up and carried him into an enclosure we'd dubbed the Little Goose Coop, where he could have food and water without competing or, more likely, a quiet place to rest and die.

To his credit, Dave was quite mature throughout the period of Arthur's decline and didn't take any opportunity for revenge. In fact, he was slow to notice that his old nemesis was not in the henhouse: in the morning, when all the hens were pressed against the gate and awaiting my arrival with the grain bucket, Dave still hung back, in a defensible position atop the nesting boxes. When he finally came out into the sun he seemed to look constantly over his shoulder.

The weather became warmer and I couldn't bear Arthur's

slow, quiet decline on the straw floor of the Little Goose Coop, with the flies clustering and buzzing about, so I brought him into the house where he could take his final, shallow breaths on the doormat. The main thing was to keep Reg, the house cat, from discovering him and submitting him to a final indignity — batting at him to see if he'd get up and play.

Once I was sure Arthur was dead I started to pluck him, so that he could live on in our feather duster, but I stopped when I had just a handful of tail feathers. It wasn't as though he had a best suit to be buried in and it seemed too undignified to put him in the ground naked. Christine dug a hole for a big rambler rose called City of York, in anticipation of the burial. I placed him in a rather nice Starbucks paper bag, appropriate because he had lived his life as if on caffeine, then carried him down to the garden and placed him gently in the bottom of the hole. Christine intoned Tennyson's *The Idylls of the King*:

"...And slowly answered Arthur from the barge:
'The old order changeth, yielding place to new,
And God fulfils himself in many ways,
Lest one good custom should corrupt the world....'"

The sun was shining, the air full of the sound of songbirds building nests, focused on bringing new life into the world.

"He was one of our first," she said, tossing a handful of earth onto him.

"We'd been here a year before we got him, remember?" We had been living in the shack, with the house under construction. I'd raised him under a heat lamp in the Little Goose Coop.

"This is not like all the lambs we've buried," she said. "They were sweet, but they hadn't lived long enough to develop personalities. But Arthur ... he was one of the originals."

In spite of myself, I felt a lump in my throat as I covered him with a couple of spadefuls of earth. Some tough farmer. That's what happens when you take an anonymous chicken out of a scrum and give him a name and some freedom.

"I've been watching Dave for the last couple of days," I said. "It's like he knows and he's taking charge." There had been more random crowing and much strutting about. "Maybe he's like a vice president and will grow into the job. Like Harry Truman — everyone thought he was a nobody in FDR's shadow."

"Dave's more like a Dan Quayle," she replied, punning brilliantly, if unintentionally.

We walked back to the house.

"Who's going to stand up to Jethro now?" Christine wondered. "Arthur ran the barnyard by force of personality. I don't think Dave's got it in him."

>—⊢◆>•◯•⊰◆⊢⊰

The whole place became Daveburg. The meek had inherited the earth.

The Buffs, true to their breed, saw that spring as an opportunity to mother. My crèche had sometimes a half dozen hens sitting in cardboard boxes full of straw. The Broody Bunch. Our supply of available eggs for eating and selling diminished drastically and our regular customers began to complain.

"Why can't I get eggs from you now? It's summer!"

"We've got too many hens on maternity leave."

"In winter they're on strike, in summer on maternity leave — sounds like you're running a welfare state."

I was glad we still had some of the Barred Rock hens, career girls with little interest in motherhood who kept our egg supply going. Although the peace and quiet in the barnyard was wonderful with just the single rooster, I began to wonder whether we should get another. In the booklet that had come with my no-tech incubator was a recommendation for one rooster to a dozen hens; we had just Dave for 25.

Among the eggs hatched a week after Arthur's death were a couple of Barred Rock chicks. He had managed to stay fertile almost to the end. One looked like a male — he was paler in colour than the others, and had a little tuft of feathers on his tail different from the pointed delta of a hen. I'll keep an eye on him, I thought.

Embraceable Ewe

For much of the year, the sheep just kept to themselves. They made their own decisions and were only vaguely aware of me and the critical role I played in their lives. Sheep have a tendency toward freethinking, the remnant of millennia spent slowly developing before primitive man discovered their wool could be made into three-piece suits. They wander the fields eating grass, lie around chewing their cud and hum "Born to Be Mild."

Although it could be argued that such a routine lacks spontaneity, to an impartial observer it doesn't seem wildly different from the life lived by most city people, who toil week-in-week-out in order to do absolutely nothing for a couple of weeks of holidays a year. But sheep don't take vacations. They don't get tired of their routine and are very well-suited to the cards life has dealt them.

From late April, when our lambs were a few weeks old, until early December, my main task was to survey the fields twice a day to determine if there were any crows circling. The lambs did have to be separated from their mothers (to wean them), which took an hour, and they did have to be wormed every two months — like cats — but otherwise, during the summer and fall, the shepherd's life was sweet. I devoted my days to raising chickens, fighting weeds in the vegetable garden and drinking gin with Christine in an old Adirondack chair beside the pond in the back pasture.

Most of the shepherding took place in the winter and very early spring when the sheep came in to a covered pen beside the barn, to eat hay and socialize. The pen was warm and calm with the animals' gentle breathing and yellow with lamplight on straw. Although to an impartial, *urban* observer this might have seemed about as interesting as watching paint dry, we often just stood around and watched them.

After the saga of Jenny, I was determined to be in charge of our flock and ruthlessly cull any that didn't make the grade. However, it didn't mean that I couldn't have my favourites. Partly as revenge against friends who were constantly showing up with boring photos of *their* children and grandchildren (telling me predictable stories about their first cuts and bruises), I carried photos of the sheep and lambs and talked incessantly about their first baby steps, their favourite bedtime story ("Little Bo Peep"), how their voices changed as they got older and so on. Soon we had fewer friends, which conformed with our desire to have a quiet life in the country. Thoreau wrote, "Simplify, simplify," and we did. (If he had really meant it he would have written it only once).

Of all the favourites, Gladys's triplets topped the list. We kept all three, and Eliza, the strong, firstborn ewe, became a superb mother — the only sheep I would ever consider cloning. Eliza had her first lamb when she was just a hogget (a fine olde English word for a yearling sheep: a teenager), followed by twins when she was just two years old. Hoggets lamb successfully about half the time and, like their human counterparts, are often more adept at getting pregnant than they are at raising the offspring. For the shepherd, this requires added supervision to ensure successful parenting.

That October we put her in with her brother Eddie. Eric had become arthritic and had gone to the great pasture in the sky, leaving his son who, rather like the romantic poets, chose to ignore the Bible's degrees of consanguinity. It's not the sort of thing you want to make a habit of, generation after generation, for even at their best sheep can be a little thick.

One gloomy afternoon the following March I went outside to check the ewes before bringing them in: several were heavily pregnant, others had new borns. An unnamed teenaged ewe was behaving strangely and seemed agitated. When I took a closer look, I saw she still had the cord-like afterbirth hanging from her. Evidently she'd lambed out in the field and had lost track of the newborn, having followed the others in, as confused young sheep are wont to do.

In the gathering dusk I searched high and low for a lost lamb, in every hollow and ditch and behind every bump of our mucky, early-spring fields, but found nothing, not a scrap of wool, a mark of blood, or any evidence of a birth. By this time it was almost completely dark, so I let all the sheep in, then went out to walk the fence line, looking for signs that a coyote had come in, grabbed the lamb and made off with it. Still nothing. Space aliens? An eagle?

Abandoning the search, I returned to the pen to find Eliza lying on the straw in labour. Her water had broken and a curious little bump in a semitransparent birth sac had already emerged. As I watched, she pushed and strained and the bump grew larger — a nose, with two hoofs positioned together beneath it (like a springboard diver) then the ears. Once the head was clear, the lamb's long, slippery body slid out easily onto the straw, breaking the umbilical cord and causing the shuddering reflex of its first breath.

I quietly approached, picked up the lamb — a girl — wiped its nose on my sleeve so that it could breathe clearly and placed it beside Eliza's head. She licked at it enthusiastically for a few minutes, then got up, turned around a few times, pawed the ground, lay down and, with more grunts and shoves, deposited onto the straw a second lamb: a boy. Again I picked up the newborn, wiped its nose and put it beside her. When she had recovered her composure and strength Eliza heaved herself onto her feet, cleaning the lambs before they got up to feed.

They were both fine, strong lambs and within 15 minutes they had struggled upright, wobbling on their long legs. Newborn Romney lambs look as if they're wearing long underwear with thick white socks pulled up above the knee. The firstborn, a few minutes ahead of her brother, made tentative steps toward her mother's bulky side and began to nudge around in her armpit, looking for the teat. Meanwhile, the boy had fallen over so Eliza turned her attention to him. She had the presence of mind to stand with a back leg splayed away from her body to make it as easy as possible for her wobbling daughter to feed.

After a few more minutes, both lambs had managed to stand and get a small amount of milk, so it was time for me to move them into a lambing pen. I picked them up, both still weak and slippery and, holding them under the belly at ground level, backed slowly toward the lambing pens. Eliza followed and within a minute or so I had the three of them safely ensconsed. It was not yet time for Eliza to rest; she continued to clean them and feed them and, with every passing moment, they became stronger and steadier on their legs.

While Eddie slumbered in the adjoining pen, a few of the ewes gathered around the lambing pen to watch, offering Eliza their congratulations before moving away. One ewe stayed, looking intently through the slats: the lambless teenager.

Suddenly Eliza dropped her head and pawed at the straw. A *third* waterbag, clear as a soap bubble, emerged. A moment later she lay down and, although crammed into the small pen with two lambs bleating and pestering her, effortlessly delivered a third. The teen and I continued to watch. Grimly I remembered the experience with Jenny and her triplets. The teen was bright-eyed and murmured quietly, her tongue occasionally darting out to lick her lips. *So that's what happened to my lamb!* she appeared to be thinking.

Maybe it *was* her lamb! Before Eliza had a chance to get up and see her third, I whipped it out of the lambing pen and placed it in front of the deprived mother. The wet newborn blinked, looked up and let out a tiny cry. The teen murmured back — a distinctive sound I had come to recognize as an ewe bonding with a lamb, so I shoved them into a lambing pen on their own.

Eliza fussed for a few minutes, knowing something had happened, but she had her hoofs full with two already, both at her for milk and care. Within a couple of hours everybody had settled down for the night, Eliza content with two lambs snuggled up against her warm bulk, the other ewe ecstatic about her "reunion."

The next day I looked in ditches and hedges that had been obscured by the gathering night, but found no trace of the lost lamb.

>-+-<+>-+-O-+-<+>-+-<

Eliza continued her stellar performance, producing nine lambs in the next three years, but she was by no means our only good ewe. Perhaps the most organized of all the sheep when it came to lambing was Notag, who could have launched a career conducting prenatal seminars. Notag was a classic Romney in that she consistently produced healthy twins (one for each available teat). She had the matter-of-fact, no-nonsense quality of her mother, Norah, but even better mothering skills. As was demonstrated one warm spring day, she also had the ability to cope with unforeseen circumstances.

Sheep choose the spot where they want to lamb. Evidently they do it well in advance, so Jan had advised me not to change the layout of feeders or lambing pens in the last month of their term. I had watched as ewes butted each other out of the way to secure the spot they wanted.

On the afternoon in question, Notag was caught by surprise. Unable to get back to the barn, she lay down in the field and put on a performance that warranted inclusion in a training video for the Farm Channel. She announced her impending labour by moving away from the others. Her ears were down and she looked rather unhappy. Occasionally, she pawed the ground. When her water broke she lay on her side, put her nose in the air, huffed and grunted for a minute or two, then delivered a lamb onto the grass. Wasting no time, she got up and stood over it, licking its nose and face.

From our position 10 yards away we saw a second waterbag emerge. How long would it be before she lay down again? She continued to lick and clean the firstborn, coaxing it to get up. Her hind legs were almost crumpling from the pressure of the second labour. Finally unable to concentrate anymore on her first lamb while standing, she lay down nose-to-nose with it in the grass. She pushed until she had the second lamb's shoulders out, all the time keeping her eyes on the wet, blinking babe in front of her. Then, in a move that could have been choreographed for a modern ballet, she got to her feet, swung around and lay down in a single graceful motion that deposited the second lamb, steaming and wet, beside its twin! Getting to her feet with an expression that said "all in a day's work", she began to clean the new lamb.

Other sheep were so stunned that labour took them completely by surprise. Once they'd expelled the misunderstood object, they often ran. This happened most frequently with teenagers, but even some of the older ones seemed to have the brains of a lawn chair when it came to mothering. The only solution was to catch the ewe, confine her with the lamb and force her to let it feed. If they bonded, all was well. If not, you were a fool to keep the ewe.

Maybe not a fool, but hardly a *real* farmer. Hobby farmers, who often were also horse owners, thought these "pet" sheep were ideal. One told me of a friend who even let hers inside the house — an appalling idea as sheep, like horses and cows, are unable to grasp the concept of bladder control. Real farmers sold bottle lambs for top dollar to hobby farmers, convinced that a bottle lamb never really knows its place.

We had only one bottle lamb: Snurgle, the orphaned runt from our first set of triplets. She was quite tame, always willing to stop for a pat as the other sheep streamed by on their way out to the fields in the morning. She had a lamb her first spring and raised it successfully. But because she was tame, she had no fear of me and was much harder to herd. She also developed an inordinate fondness for groceries, probably spurred on by my early, Dr. Spock-influenced attentions, and shoved more worthy sheep aside at the feeder, hoovering up any remaining grain after the others had eaten their fill.

Having become fat during the summer, she couldn't get pregnant in the fall, but regardless, all winter she ate enough for two or three, as did the rest of the pregnant ewes. Every 17 days (the ovulation cycle for ewes) she stared through the fence at her brother. He was driven so mad by lust he practically uprooted the wooden fence posts and pen to get to her. But despite his best efforts she wouldn't "settle" into her pregnancy. Instead she grew fatter and fatter as fall turned into winter and then spring. I could have separated her from the others, but she would have bawled like a spoiled child locked in her room, sheep being sociable creatures.

In the spring, after all the lambs were born and the ewes had thinned down, one sheep stood out. Like a fleecy seal, Snurgle lumbered around looking for more grass while the others lay quietly and chewed their cud. She could, I suppose, have been barbecued, but only with the fire department on standby. If I didn't thin her down, she'd either die of a heart attack and I'd be unable to dig a hole big enough to bury her, or I'd go through the same thing again next winter. I used electrified fencing wire to create a Fat Farm compound and dragged her into it. She bawled for days and resumed a diet of straw and water. I kept the gate locked so that representatives of the SPCA couldn't get in.

Gradually she began to reemerge from beneath the smooth cocoon of blubber. I was considering allowing her to rejoin the flock when a local farmer, Mel, dropped by to talk about the quantity of hay I wanted to buy for the winter. An old shepherd who had once managed a large flock on an English estate, he cast a practised eye over the solitary sheep in the electric pen.

"What's she quarantined for? She sick?" he asked.

"That's my Fat Farm!" I announced proudly. "She didn't lamb this year. I'm taking some weight off her so she'll breed in the fall."

"Whaaaaat?" he exclaimed. He made a *phweeet* sound and jerked his thumb over his shoulder in a she's-outta-here gesture. "Take her to the auction! She'll never be right again! Why would you want to feed her all winter?"

"She's a pet!" I protested. "Nice fleece, too."

"Oh, hell, you want a pet, go pick one of the good ones in the field and hand-feed her. It'll take you a couple of days, but you won't be feeding a freeloader."

Mel began to talk about his early days in the valley, when he had made extra money as an itinerant shearer.

"You wouldn't be the first to pass off a sheep like that as a pregnant ewe — there's bound to be somebody at the auction who wouldn't know the difference," he said. "Talk about buyer beware! In the old days, shepherds castrated their ram lambs and when their fleece had grown out, after about five months, they'd take them to the auction and sell them as ewes because they'd go for a higher price. I'd shear some of these 'pregnant ewes' just taking off the belly wool, when whoa! I'd nick the pecker!"

"I shouldn't have any trouble finding someone who wants their grass cut, or a companion for a goat or horse," I muttered.

"Whatever," he said skeptically and went back to talking about his son who preferred exercising at the fitness club to helping with the haymaking.

Molly the Broiler

➤·⟨⟩·O·⟨⟩·⟨

We live in a "recreational" countryside, where horses are like RVs. Most of our neighbours own them or board them for owners in the city. No one can understand why we don't have them too. I've been told that some people actually take pleasure in owning horses; they even get to ride them once in a while when they aren't brushing them, feeding them, cleaning up after them, calling the vet, or working to pay all the bills. But to an unbiased observer there's no practical *use* for them, unlike in France where the *chevaline* wagon is a popular feature of local markets.

The last time I got on a horse was about 25 years ago, in an era in which I had a girlfriend who wasn't content to hang out, but instead wanted to *do* things. One of the adventures she proposed for an otherwise restful Sunday involved driving out to a riding stable on the grassy edge of a tidal mudflat along the coast. In our blue jeans and windbreakers, we climbed aboard a couple of bored hayburners and trailed out of the paddock with a half dozen other greenhorns. Led by a guide sporting a Real Cowboy Hat, we rode single-file along a narrow trail winding through the sand dunes. As I recall, it was a beautiful summer day, a breeze blowing off the sea and rippling the long grasses.

The pace was restful, too, after our busy week in the city. The horse's back-and-forth, rhythmic motion, the sound of its hooves — *dah-dunk, dah-dunk* — on the packed trail ... (I imagined covered wagons behind me, scouts on the lookout and ole Clem was playin' a lonesome refrain on his harmonica.)

We pulled up at a slight rise. The guide turned in his saddle and addressed his posse, his voice awaking me. "You're on your own from here," he said. "You can let 'em run if you want. Be back at the stables in a half hour."

All the horses' nostrils began to flare and even the most sway-backed of them stiffened. With a "Yee-haaa!" our guide tore off down the trail. The horses, with their urban cargo, hesitated for just a second and then took off as well. It didn't matter what the riders wanted — this was their favourite part of the day. All of a sudden we were galloping over open beach. It was fun, although it reminded me, ominously, of my first time on a bicycle, hurtling downhill. I believed my girlfriend was right behind me, but when I finally got the courage to yank my head around I couldn't spot her anywhere. Crying "Whoa, Silver!" I pulled hard on the reins, skidded to a stop and turned the beast around.

She was near some trees on the edge of the beach, about 100 yards away.

"What's happening?" I called. "You okay?"

"Damned horse is trying to knock me off!" she yelled back. The horse was making passes at a tree, standing back, eyeing another with a low bough.

"Here I come!" I called, or something equally confidence-inspiring. A chance to rescue my lady love! I slackened my grip on the reins and kicked the horse in the ribs as hard as I could, which wasn't all that hard as I was wearing hippie sandals. My horse took off as if launched from a slingshot. Forty yards, 30 yards — we were galloping like the wind.

Suddenly, the horse faltered in the wind and went down on its knees. I sailed off, doing a half flip and landing almost on my head in the gumbo. When I regained my balance I was absolutely coated in a slime that turned my hair to dreadlocks. My girlfriend and her horse ceased their struggle, it distracted by her fits of laughter. My horse got up, we shook ourselves off and, with as much dignity as we could muster, made our way back to the stables.

"You all come back now!" said the cheery woman at the gate, blithely disregarding my sudden transformation. Not likely. The reality of my narrow escape had sunk in. I never got on a horse again. When we moved to the country, I did briefly entertain the idea of buying a Sicilian donkey that I could ride bareback on the equestrian trails in the nearby park, my toes dragging behind and cutting two furrows in the wood-chip path, just to annoy the horse people. But as with all my good ideas (including winning the lottery), I've just never gotten around to it.

>–·–·–·—O—·–·–·—<

Sharon, a country neighbour who had moved from the city years before to indulge her passion for horses, taught at a school nearby and, it appeared to our jaundiced eyes, spent every nickel on her animals. Sharon loved them all: two horses, six cats, a parakeet named Rosie and two dogs. When she first moved to the country, before she was able to secure the teaching position, she worked as an assistant for Willem, the local veterinarian. How else could she have afforded all those critters, those shots, those visits?

Sharon was the sort of person who could not ignore an abandoned or wounded animal, a real problem in urban-shadow areas. When people get tired of a pet or their circumstances change, last Christmas's puppy or Easter's bunny goes for a car ride and is dumped on a country road. I was aware of this and couldn't deal with it, so I gave guilt-money to the SPCA. Sharon, however, felt compelled to stop and help.

One night, travelling home on a dark country road, her headlights picked up two pairs of eyes — palm-size tabby kittens. She took them home, fed them and, when the time came, had them spayed at Willem's after hours, acting as OR nurse herself to keep the costs down. They joined the gang, and so it went. Occasionally an animal died (usually of old age) and she grieved deeply at the loss, but otherwise her ark was trouble-free.

When Sharon had to go away for a few days I offered to look after her menagerie. I took a particular interest in feeding the horses, walking them between the barn and the paddock and catering to their every whim. I thought that if I spent time around them I could conquer my fear, my suspicion that they relished the fact they could squash me like a bug. But I couldn't get over my anxiety. They were big and heavy and skittish. Short of being reincarnated as a horse — as *Sharon's* horse — I wanted nothing more to do with the species.

In the name of friendship, Sharon did her best not to comment on *our* farm practices. I knew she thought we were heartless to sell our lambs for meat and to raise chickens to fill the freezer. She would rather prevent an animal from breeding than end up having to kill or cull its offspring. Raised as a carnivore, she had gradually evolved into a vegetarian, like her horses, although she didn't mind spooning out huge tins of mystery meat for her dogs and cats. For our part, we were disgusted by the wet pet food, yet fed our chickens all sorts of sludge from the fridge and tolerated their penchant for picking through the sheep manure in search of undigested grain. Sharon did like the sheep, however, and briefly contemplated giving our old ram, Eric, a dignified retirement. Then she realized he would be harassed by her dogs. The chickens she found rather charming but, when I pointed out that they were not really pets, but were, in fact, feathered reptiles (like all birds) who didn't like to be handled or stroked, she seemed to lose interest.

Probably just to be meddlesome, I set myself a personal goal:

Sharon must have chickens. Although it was none of my business, I thought she needed some *real* farm animals at her place, and besides, she could use the eggs. It was tit for tat: she thought we were crazy not to have horses or dogs, we thought she was nuts to go through life without poultry. Whenever I saw her, I talked about how even-tempered and useful the purebred hens were, how long they lived. "Yeah, yeah," she responded, slightly annoyed, brushing aside the suggestion.

Then one day she phoned to say she had been driving home from school when she saw something in the ditch. "Looked like feathers. White ones. I had to stop and *oh, man*.... It was one of those broiler chickens. It must've fallen off the back of a truck...."

"It was probably on the way to the slaughterhouse," I interjected. Trucks packed with broiler chickens were a common sight.

"It was still alive... but one wing was twisted and broken. I just couldn't leave it, so I put it in my truck and brought it home." Her voice broke; she was almost in tears. I thought she was going to ask me to come over and kill it, but I should have known better. Her voice suddenly brightened.

"So I called Willem and he sounded a little skeptical, but said to bring her over and he'd have a look. It was fascinating. Willem really got into it. He called a couple of other vets to find out how much anaesthetic to give a chicken. You know, in all his years as a vet, he'd never operated on a chicken...."

I wonder why? A neighbour had taken her children's pet chicken to the vet when it had become old and sick. The vet, who had been forewarned of the children's impending trauma, gravely carried the chicken "into the examining room" while they waited outside. After several minutes, during which he probably went out back for a smoke, he returned to the waiting room and told the children that the chicken had to stay with him for a day or two. When the chicken "died on the operating table," the children accepted the news and the parents avoided calling the grief counsellors.

"She's a bit scuffed up from hitting the road and she's got a splint on her wing, but I've got her in the kitchen where she's eating some dry cat food!" Sharon finished.

"She's a girl. That's good," I said, desperate to say something positive.

"Why is it good she's a girl?"

"Well...uh...they don't grow as fast as the males and they're a lot less aggressive."

It was time to educate Sharon about poultry. I told her about the broilers we raised, how fast they grew, what their life expectancy was. Broilers are meat birds, while hybrid layers live caged in batteries and supply the standard supermarket egg. The reality of life on these factory farms is an argument for vegetarianism. Broilers have enormous appetites and grow very fast, but the inbreeding gives them genetic mutations, the most visible of which is twisted toes. Like circus clowns, their feet are so big that they can only walk rather than run like normal chickens. If one grew in proportion to its feet, it would be as big as a turkey. Their main value is in becoming three-pound frying chickens (the boneless chicken breast on the foam tray in the supermarket) after ingesting seven weeks of hormone-laced feed that may contain "animal by-products."

Sharon appeared oblivious to my practical turn of mind. "I think she's really cute, though I haven't named her yet. Will she lay eggs?" she asked.

"Possibly a few, about the size of a Ping-Pong ball," I sighed.

"Oh, well, that doesn't matter. But listen, the reason I'm calling, other than to tell you all this good news, is because I'm worried that she doesn't have a companion of the same species. Have you got a hen or two I could buy?"

At the time, we were a bit low on hens and having trouble producing enough eggs to satisfy our city customers. We did have one old hen (I was going to turn her into soup because she wasn't earning her keep), the last of the hybrid layer pullets we had bought when we first moved to the farm. This charming character had earned the name Patsy Cline due to her habit of crooning in a minor key. We had long since moved into purebreds and become so sophisticated in our poultry management that poor Patsy no longer justified her spot on the perch.

"I've got one you can *have*," I replied. "You'll be saving it from the soup pot. As long as you don't mind getting only the occasional egg."

We agreed that Christine and I would go for coffee the following morning and bring Patsy along. That night, while all the chickens were asleep, I got Patsy off the perch and put her in the portable cage the kitty uses when he goes to Willem's. In the morning, after breakfast and chores, the three of us went for a ride.

At Sharon's gate we were greeted by her throng of bounding, drooling, barking dogs. Her two originals had died of old age and she had replaced them with an unspayed Samoyed-cross bitch from one of the local "no-kill" animal shelters. Gretel unerringly found the weak spot in the fence in order to greet next door's German shepherd. The result: 11 puppies. Sharon doggedly set about finding good homes for all of them and was down to four big puppies by the time we arrived with Patsy. She had reduced the litter to two but, as she had guaranteed she would take back any of them that bit babies or otherwise didn't bond with their adoptive families, she was back up to four. "It's only temporary," she'd replied when I told her she'd gone completely mad.

We lifted Patsy's cage out of the back of the truck and, holding it high above the leaping hounds, fought our way to the door.

The baying increased as they picked up the scent of the cowering hen. A horse watched the chaotic scene with a bemused expression, its head protruding through the top of the Dutch door of the barn and a couple of cats skulked in the shadows.

There was no mechanical doorbell, as there was no need for one. When we made it to the landing, Sharon held the door open wide enough for us to squeeze in single-file, meanwhile shouting, "Get back! Out!" at the dogs. A tall, lean woman with cropped, hennaed hair (the better to fit under a riding helmet), she looked surprisingly serene in her anarchic home. I caught a glimpse of Patsy inside the cage; her beak was open and she seemed to be panting.

We kicked off our boots and rounded the corner into Sharon's kitchen. There, on a sheet of newspaper on the floor, sat her bionic chicken, a bird seemingly assembled from spare parts. Like all broilers, she had trouble sitting comfortably on her great big yellow feet and looked to be in danger of tipping over backward, like a downhill skier in a squatting position. Her feathers were dishevelled, partly from the road burn and stress, partly because broilers never seem to learn to groom themselves. Her hurt wing was taped to her body and, when she got up, she flapped the other one halfheartedly for balance. Her comb was only a small ridge of skin just beginning to redden, a sign that she was not yet mature. She was probably only seven weeks old, the age when commercial broilers get the one-way ride to the plant, and weighed perhaps five pounds including feathers, beak and clown feet.

"This is Molly," Sharon announced triumphantly, gesturing at her newly named patient. Molly the Broiler. "The dogs have been banished until she's well enough to go out to the barn — that's why they're so crazy."

"How are the cats taking all this?" Christine asked.

"Oh, fine. Everyone is except for Rosie. She's camped out on the showerhead and shitting into the bathtub."

"What's in the bowl?" I asked, referring to the contents of the dog dish beside Molly.

"I went and got some layer pellets at the co-op yesterday after talking to you," she replied. "That's the ticket, right?"

"Probably. Her best chance of a long life is if you slow down her growth rate. She'll eat herself to death if you feed her on anything too rich."

Christine had walked over to a windowsill to stroke a sleeping cat who was apparently indifferent to all the fuss. It was Judith, one of the kitties rescued from the roadside a couple of years earlier. She'd seen it all, I guessed.

"Let Patsy out, I'm sure she's hungry," said Sharon.

With the cage pointed toward the dog dish, I opened its door and stood back. After a moment, a keen-eyed, russet-feathered, red-combed head appeared. It swivelled around to check out the terrain. One foot emerged, then the second and with two more purposeful steps Patsy was at the dog dish. *Tok-tok-tok*, her beak rhythmically hit the plastic. There was a lot of food in the dish, more than I would put out for a couple of chickens. I wondered if Patsy was going to demonstrate that *any* chicken, given a chance, could binge and die. *Tok-tok-tok*. Her crop, the sac where she stores grain to release slowly into her gizzard for grinding and digesting, began to swell. *Tok-tok-tok*. Finally, with her crop swollen like a balloon, she stopped, stepped to the water jug, drank deeply, then began to look around. A louse or a flea bit her and she swivelled her head around, burying her beak in her tail feathers. Spying the windowsill, she marched over and with a single graceful flap of her wings flew onto it. Judith looked up sleepily. Patsy strode the few steps to the cat and gave her a sharp peck on the head, then turned and gazed out the window. The cat jumped down. Patsy dropped a large white-and-black pile of shit onto the sill.

Sharon was delighted. "She's so beautiful and so agile compared to Molly. This is great! Look at the way she moves!" Sharon got out some coffee cups and we sat down at the kitchen table. Molly roused herself and, swaying slightly, began to peck up the few remaining pellets.

>-!-◆-○-◆-!-<

A couple of weeks later I called Sharon to check on her chickens. Molly had recovered completely and regained the use of her wing but, being a broiler, she could use it only for balance. Patsy had terrorized all the cats, but had made only one foray outside, through the cat door, where she had narrowly missed being eaten. Sharon had converted a corner of her horse barn into a chicken area and was preparing to move the chickens out of the house and let the dogs back in so that everything could, in her terms, return to normal. With her innate, gypsy-like empathy, she could approach both chickens and pet them without getting pecked. To my delight, she announced that she wanted more.

"This time get some real ones," I told her. "No more broilers or old hens. How about a rooster? The dogs might learn to leave the chickens alone if you had a rooster."

Sharon had always liked Arthur, rightly perceiving him to be a romantic character. We had a young rooster named Ben of whom Christine had grown very fond (not unlike Lucky), but whom Arthur was determined to run out of town.

One night I lifted Ben and a couple of Barred Rock pullets off the perch, put them into my portable chicken cage and took them over to Sharon's. She named the two Barred Rocks after nuns at the convent school she had attended as a child. The permanent dog pack had grown from two to six, as she had given up trying to find homes for the rejected pups. Willem and Sharon had spent a couple of evenings spaying and neutering. Rosie the parakeet had come to terms with the interlopers and gone back to her old habit of flying around inside the house, shitting randomly instead of just into the bathtub. Molly and Patsy were happily ensconced in the barn and were occasionally let out into the yard under supervision. Patsy always made a beeline for the cat door at the house to clean up anything left in their dishes in the kitchen.

Ben and the pullets fit right in, understanding chaos to be the natural order of things. Sharon was pleased with the whole situation, at least in part, I'm sure, because she was demonstrating to me that you needn't be a control freak in order to have a happy flock.

As it turned out, Molly the Broiler only lived another year, reaching the size of a young turkey before she succumbed to a heart attack. Patsy lived on for another year before expiring, probably egg-bound in a last heroic effort to earn her keep. Sharon sailed through it all with only brief sorrow — although she still treated the chickens as pets, she had become more philosophical about their brief lives and the limitations of doctoring them. Besides, she'd become used to having the eggs.

Loretti the Training Sheep

One winter day, after we'd been on the farm for a couple of years, the phone rang (actually, it had rung quite a number of times since we moved). It was our fellow shepherd, Karen, who had bought Mary's Girl a few months earlier to add some new blood to her flock of a half dozen Heinz 57 ewes.

She called to offer us one of hers, pregnant by her old ram Laszlo. Laszlo had serviced the flock for generations and had become a family pet, despite charging and flattening both Karen's husband and her son on various occasions. You don't turn your back on a ram, especially if you're male.

"Which one?" I asked. I knew her flock fairly well.

"The black-faced ewe with ... well, one of the black ewes. She's hard to describe. She's got a fleece that's brown on the tips and smoky grey-blue closer to the skin."

Although the coloured fleece sounded attractive, and apparently commanded premium prices from spinners and handweavers, I was slightly suspicious. Karen's flock had become so inbred that she had traded common sense for uncommon wool. On the other hand, we didn't have any coloured sheep (or sheep of colour, in the current parlance). Our flock were white or, rather, *beige*, it being the old word for an unwashed, natural-coloured fleece.

"Sure, why not?" I said, knowing that, at the very least, her flock was healthy. We agreed on $100.

A few days later Karen arrived at the gate in her old Toyota pickup. Under the canopy I could see an agitated, pacing sheep, its hoofs making a racket on the rusty deck audible above the engine noise and the burbling exhaust. As the sheep trotted from one side to the other, the truck rocked on its springs.

Karen was out of breath and seemed agitated herself. "This wasn't the one I wanted, but it's the only one we could catch," she puffed. Her son had helped her lift the beast onto the tailgate and push it under the canopy. "You can have her for $50...," she said, her voice trailing off.

I peered through the cab's windows. A pair of staring yellow eyes met mine. The beast attached to them was breathing rapidly, like sheep in a horror movie. The pupil of a sheep's eye is a dark horizontal band across the middle of the eyeball; this one had an alien, challenging gaze, different from the soft-brown, deferential look of our purebred Romneys.

"Is this a Romney?" I asked, trying to sound conversational.

"She's got some Cheviot in her, plus the Romney," said Karen. I didn't know much about other sheep breeds, but I suspected Cheviots were not mild-tempered (like Chevys).

"I ... I was trying to breed in the Cheviot to clean the wool off their legs and faces so they'd be easier to shear," she said, sounding distinctly defensive. She had a point. Romneys *are* very woolly, their small round ears can look rather like those of bears. If you don't give them a haircut about six to eight months after they've been shorn, they can go wool-blind. I could see the logic behind the cross-breeding, but I didn't want the wool pulled over *my* eyes. Nevertheless, I didn't feel I could reject the ewe; Karen had had such a struggle. I got into the back of the truck with a rope halter, wrestled it onto the ewe and dragged her out.

Before too long she had fallen in with the rest of the gang. The new one, however, was a more solitary animal and we often found her on her own. She also seemed to be more of a browser than a grazer. Like a goat, she would chew at the leaves of any plant, seeking the next great taste sensation. She couldn't be put into an area with shrubs as she rarely ate only what she was standing on.

A couple of months later this still-unnamed, restless, rather difficult sheep lay down in the straw and delivered a black girl lamb into the cold, damp springtime air. Fortunately the birth went without incident, as the new mum was skittish whenever I was nearby. Motherhood didn't calm her down; she baaed constantly, with a harsh croak like a smoker's cough. She pawed the ground aggressively around the baby, occasionally bashing it on the head with a sharp-hoofed, manure-laden foot. But the lamb grew well and was, according to our city friends, even cuter than the white ones. She had nubbly black wool like a Berber carpet, black skin and even a black tongue. All our visitors wanted to cuddle her, until they saw her staring yellow eyes.

Christine, with her talent for the obscure, named her Loretti, so that ever after she could have this conversation with guests:

"What's her name?"

"Loretti!"

"Why'd you name her that?"

"Uh, the movie 'Coal Miner's Daughter'... you know, Loretta Lynn?"

"Whatever."

Loretti was two weeks old when the Romney ewes started lambing and the arrival of new lambs aroused an aggressive streak in her mother. When she began to butt some of the newborns out of her way, I grabbed her and Loretti and stuck them into the adjoining pen, where Eddie lived for the 11 months of the year when he wasn't at work. The smell of impending birth arouses a ram to the same fever pitch as the breeding cycle, making it difficult — not to mention dangerous — to help the ewes. He remained separated, though able to gaze through the fence at them, until five months before the day we wanted to start lambing.

Eddie was quite happy with the companionship and, every morning, the three of them went out a different gate into a side field that I had fenced the previous summer.

As everything seemed to be moving along smoothly, I busied myself with indoor tasks and only emerged to put out water and feed late in the afternoon. One day, I had my boots on and was just pulling on my coat when, out of the corner of my eye, I saw a woolly black convoy flash past me.

I wheeled around and saw Eddie and Loretti's mother running hard, some small creatures in pursuit. I ran out the door, vaulted a fence and sprinted as fast as I could in my gumboots toward the side field, yelling. Someone else was yelling too, calling and whistling from down the road.

In 10 seconds I was at the scene. Loretti was on her back, two Jack Russell terriers at her throat. Eddie and the ewe milled about by the far fence; like all sheep, their only defensive strategy was flight. As I thundered over, bellowing like a banshee, one of the Jack Russells backed away, snarling, but the other stayed on Loretti's throat until I kicked it on the side of the head, pushing it off few feet. Both dogs promptly backed along the ditch line, then began to run toward the road. A couple there were calling the dogs, which I realized had squeezed through a spot where the fence crosses the ditch — a gap far too small for any coyote, the only natural predator.

I picked up Loretti, who had gone into shock, her eyes glazed and half shut, and pressed my fingers over the puncture wounds in her neck. Christine had emerged from the house, having heard all the yelling.

"Grab the keys," I shouted. "We've got to get to the vet!"

We hurtled down the driveway, Christine at the wheel. At the gate stood a middle-aged couple, quite well dressed, each holding a terrier. "Run them over!" I commanded Christine, but she ignored me.

The man was frozen, immobile, not knowing what we'd do.

"We're sorry! We're sorry!" cried the woman. "We just moved here!"

"*Ever heard of a leash?*" I bellowed. That, at least, was the gist of it. "You think you can move to the country and let your dogs run free?" I held up the lamb. Blood had begun to seep between my fingers clamped around her neck.

"Here," she exclaimed, holding her terrier out toward me. "You kill him! He's yours!" The terrier snarled at me.

"I'm calling the pound!" I shouted. If it were possible to die of adrenalin poisoning, I'd have been finished. Christine pulled the wheel around and sped away, regrettably not fast enough to shower them with gravel.

Willem the vet was only a mile away and, fortunately, he was not engaged in cosmetic surgery on a Doberman or some other pressing task. After his many years of erasing skid marks from dogs and cats, he could tell right away that Loretti's life wasn't in danger. I began to calm down. He snipped a little of the bloody wool away from the wounds, put on some antiseptic cream, wound a large bandage around her neck like a turtleneck, gave her a shot of antibiotics in the rump and handed her back to me with a bill for $25.

At home, hungry lamb reunited with mother, everything calmed down. After calling the pound, which also does predator control for farmers to keep them from shooting at anything that moves (this is a Canadian farm, after all), I began a systematic check of the fences, plugging any hole large enough for a rat to go through. Bucolic Killara Farm was becoming Fort Killara.

Loretti scarcely skipped a beat, although I felt *I* had aged years. I hated the thought of losing any animals to predators, especially dogs. The man from the pound reported that he had tracked down the people with the Jack Russells, but there was nothing he could do.

"Why?" I asked, my hackles rising. Was it my responsibility to fence domestic predators *out*, rather than their owners' to fence them *in*?

"Coyotes got 'em."

"The dogs *and* their owners?" I asked hopefully.

"Just the dogs."

"Rats."

"Sorry, you gotta deal with rodents yourself," he answered laconically, making light of a grim situation.

With her white turtleneck, Loretti was easier to spot in the dark and when I removed the bandage a week later the wounds were healing well. She grew fast and I weaned her at three months, by which time she weighed about 50 pounds, her face and legs still bare and black, but her body now wearing a rusty-brown wool coat. She began to turn grey at the tips of her fleece and, when you parted the wool on her back, you could see it was dark brown all the way down to her black skin. A hand-spinner who bought her first fleece swore she'd come back every year.

But the lamb's temperament wasn't much better than her mother's. If I walked into the field or the pen and Loretti and her mother were nearby, they'd promptly run and then all the other sheep would run too (because they're sheep). Usually the flock got used to me in the winter and let me walk among them, but now they were restless and agitated in my presence. This was a management problem. When friends came by and wanted to see the sheep, we couldn't get close.

One day when I was discussing some lambs for market with Dave Thompson, the livestock broker with a "Ewe Haul" van, I asked him if he'd take Loretti's mother, too.

"Won't get much for it," he said.

"She's got a nice fleece," I countered.

"Who cares?"

She went anyway, but even without her mother's influence Loretti became more and more crochety as the months went by. If sheep gave concerts, Loretti would have played drums for a heavy-metal band. In the spring, when the grass was at its richest, she ate so much that she looked like a burro with panniers. And she had an oddly small cloven hoof with a space between the toes exactly the size of all the sharp field stones, so she frequently limped. She was *difficult*; she didn't fit in. Perhaps, we thought hopefully, motherhood would mellow her. After seeing Eddie woo her, I put a mark on the calendar for 147 days hence.

A ewe gives birth somewhere between 145 and 150 days after her encounter with the ram. At 145 days I started watching Loretti, but couldn't tell if she was any more restless than usual; at 147, she began to *baa* in a rasping voice; at 148, she lay down and gave signs of going into labour, but ... nothing. A watched ewe never lambs, so I thought I'd give it another day. Day 149, I called Jan.

"Better pull it," he said, "or you'll lose the ewe, too."

Christine and I put on our lamb-pulling togs, which are even grubbier than our normal farm clothes, and headed down to the barn. I cornered Loretti and lunged for her as she tried to thunder by me. As gently as I could, I wrestled her to the ground. Christine crouched at her head, putting most of her weight on her neck, and held the lower of her two front feet off the ground to limit her ability to get up and make a run for it.

I got a hand into the back of her and a couple of inches inside ran into a nose: must be a stuck lamb. Working my hand around and past it, I began to feel for jammed knees as Loretti thrashed and puffed, her yellow eyes wild, her nostrils flared. Christine used her meagre weight to hold the beast down. The lamb was huge and dead. As most ewes expect twins and are fed accordingly, a ewe with a single lamb sometimes has problems.

Loretti was exhausted and we weren't much better off. To make matters worse, she appeared to have a prolapsed uterus, which I fixed after consulting the sheep book, and an infection, probably from my rough farmer's hands. I put her into a lambing pen by herself and we played doctor for a few days until she was well again.

That was the thing about Loretti — she was an educational tool. Those shepherds who have only quality livestock never learn the difficult techniques of animal husbandry. I considered offering her to the local 4-H club.

TRAINING SHEEP FOR SALE
U-LEARN IT ALL
MURPHY'S LAW-CERTIFIED
TO GOOD FARM ONLY

However, I got busy, Loretti did her best to remain unnoticed, and before long it was fall and breeding season again, time for Eddie's annual visit to the flock. This time Loretti didn't seem to "settle," and every 17 days was back for more. Eventually it dawned on me that she *couldn't* get pregnant, which I surmised was due to her prolapse and infection; she was probably sterile from the ewe's equivalent of childbed fever. As the price we got for her coloured fleece paid for her feed for the winter, I decided she could stay on as Eddie's companion — like a wether, the castrated rams that farmers used to keep when wool prices were high.

Once again fate had provided a practical solution. Loretti and Eddie became constant and, it seemed, platonic companions.

That spring lambs were born as usual and, certain that our job here was done, we booked tickets for England in July. There would be sheep there, too, but if I became bored we could while away the days in galleries, restaurants, gardens and other tourist attractions.

A couple of city friends, Robert and Audrey, had long expressed an interest in caretaking if we were ever away. Robert had been in business and Audrey was the spinner and weaver who had bought Loretti's birthday suit; both had travelled extensively in the country, but had never had the experience of managing a menagerie of sheep and chickens. They came out for a crash course in who-goes-where, who-eats-what and where-to-find-the-eggs and discovered what we had been maintaining all along — the animals knew what they were supposed to do, especially in the summer. They had a routine and were therefore easy to look after. Robert and Audrey could watch them graze if they wished. The sheep spent their time in the fields and hung around in the shade with the saltblock and the automatic waterer. Nevertheless, I left a page of notes and Jan's phone number in case of an emergency.

And away we went.

Their idyllic two weeks on the farm went well until the penultimate day. A thunderstorm had hit early in the morning and Robert, concerned that sheep might be like horses and get spooked by thunder and wind (they don't), went down to check on them. To his horror, he found Loretti cleaning a newborn black lamb. He ran back to the house and called Jan.

"Has she had a drink yet?" Jan asked.

"No, but I have."

"Of milk? That's the important thing. Watch her," Jan instructed.

"Anything else?"

"Find some iodine and sterilize the umbilical cord and call

me back in a few hours if she appears listless." Jan would have made a good GP.

We heard all this, of course, when we got back, by which time Loretti's lamb was flourishing and Robert and Audrey's crisis had turned into a good story. The lamb was a tiny, eager boy, who had already figured out, and survived, his mother's latest idiosyncrasy: her two teats were set at the back of the udder, so it was easiest for him to feed standing behind her, directly in the path of her excretions. There was no way we were going to keep him and thus breed Loretti's personality into a whole flock of ewes, so I casually mentioned to Christine one day that I was going to ship him with the rest of the late-fall market lambs.

"What will Audrey and Robert say? You can't do that! They ask about him every time we see them."

"We could lie."

"No way! You've got to find him a home."

Though the sheep-buying business is truly *caveat emptor*, I couldn't in all honesty sell him as a breeder. However, fate once again intervened. Karen's Laszlo toppled over in the pasture and had to be dragged off, hoofs-first. I phoned her.

"We're looking for a home for that little ram lamb born while we were away. Christine won't let me sell him for sausage."

"He's quite small, isn't he?"

"Yeah," I said defensively. As the ram's size helps determine the carcass size of his offspring, most shepherds want a big one.

"That might work out for us," she said, to my amazement. "Our sheep are too big to handle now, so a small one would suit us quite well."

Christine, Audrey and Robert were pleased the lamb had a job. A few days later he went in the pickup truck up to Karen's, baaing all the way. He grew out fairly well, although never anywhere near the size of his dad, had many children and is

still alive today, although Karen complains every spring about
the bruises on her legs. He butts the hand that feeds, just like
his mother. He's known as Omar, if you ever happen to be by
that way.

Loretti also lived on and in the two subsequent years had two
breech births. But by then I was ready for her and had all my
antennae up as she approached her delivery date. Instead of
waiting too long, as we had done with her first lamb, I caught
her promptly, dragged her down, Christine lay on her head
and I pulled the lamb. Assisting in a breech birth is a bit like
solving a puzzle. Once when I had rummaged inside the ewe
but felt nothing, not a hoof, a knee, an ear or a nose, to give
me any idea of what was going on, I had realized that what I
was touching when I had my arm in so far that the tideline was
nearly at my elbow, was a lamb's back. I had worked my hand
around until I found what I hoped was a back leg, straight-
ened it carefully, trying not to cut the uterine wall with the
hoof, and positioned it along the birth canal. I found the
other leg and did the same thing, trying not to squeeze off
the umbilical cord. Once the two hind hooves were out I
pulled hard, rocking the unborn lamb from side to side to
clear its ribcage and get it out as quickly as possible. You have
to pull fast when they're coming out backward because, as
soon as the umbilical cord breaks, the lamb will take a breath
and its head, of course, is still in the watery world of the
womb.

Both lambs survived. The first was a boy that grew up as a market
lamb. He had a beautiful fleece and hide with thick brown
wool, which I tanned with a mixture of alum and salt (as described
in Christine's *Australian Country Women's Coronation Cookbook*,
published for Edward VIII's aborted coronation in 1937).

The second lamb, in the second year, announced its impending arrival by showing only its tail. By that time we were blasé about the process and pulled the lamb with casual expertise. This time, however, Loretti had produced a girl, a black lamb with, we hoped, a portion of good, stable Romney blood in her.

As I pulled it, chanting, "Be alive, be alive," and brought it around to Loretti's head, Christine let go her death grip and staggered to her feet. Loretti stirred, grunted, got up quickly, then turned and began to lick the newborn. Christine and I looked at each other with a single thought, *Why do we put up with this every year?*

"We're going to cull Loretti," I said. "Three out of four years now we've had to pull the lamb."

I got no argument from her and began to look for Dave Thompson's phone number.

Wild Things

In the hedges along the front of the property and in the rough grass on the edge of the pasture, lived voles, pheasants and bunnies that provided food for the smaller predators, including feral cats and the barn owl, and culinary diversity for the coyotes when they ran out of lapdogs and house cats in the neighbourhood. Every time a hand-made poster with a photocopied picture of a pet dog — usually being throttled by a bright-eyed, happy child — went up on the power pole at the corner, or a neighbour came by asking us to keep an eye out for Fluffy who hadn't come home the night before, I thought, *There but for yours go mine*, or words to that effect.

We sought a balance between the agricultural and the natural. The "agricultural" was represented by our sheep and chickens, much sought after by the representatives of the natural contingent, notably the coyotes that lurked just outside the property, waiting for me to drop my guard or stay out too late drinking and carousing to lock the animals in for the night.

Neighbours were divided about what to do with the invaders. Those with only horses or cattle had a live-and-let-live attitude, probably because their own livestock weren't threatened, while the owners of mild-mannered animals such as sheep and chickens tended to take a more aggressive stance. After the loss of a couple of chickens to coyotes, and the near-death experience of Loretti from the invading Jack Russells, I began to turn Killara Farm into a fortress by improving what the agriculture department pamphlets called Field Management Devices. I cut hedges back to the property line, built wire fencing and let the hedges grow back. Along another property line, which ended at the woods, I installed an electric line to power a roll of "Electronet" fencing set just inside the permanent fence. Most self-respecting coyotes like to dig underneath fences at night, and I figured that if one had its belly on the damp ground, then touched the electric wire with its wet nose, I'd be able to read a newspaper by its bright light.

There was a weak spot along one fence line, shared by another neighbour's back property, but as they had a couple of dogs that roamed a yard near the front of the house I felt my boundary was secure. Although I tried very hard not to be sentimental about our livestock, I took it personally when one was killed by anything that wasn't airborne. I felt negligent. Besides, it was tough digging holes in the heavy clay soil to bury any "mortalities".

The new wire fencing was called "Field and Farm," a vast improvement on the rusty old barbed wire. It was a grid of horizontal and vertical wires, with the spaces near the bottom much smaller than the ones near the top, thus good for restraining small critters like chickens and lambs. An acquaintance who owned horses, and in general was a bit of a know-it-all, warned me that the lambs would get their heads stuck in it, but that never happened. The only time a lamb got its head stuck was in the vertical bars of a hay feeder.

>─┤◆>─O─‹◆┤─<

Seeking more pasture and fewer predators, I had once contemplated getting goats to clean up an area of bramble and weed in a low spot I thought I could reclaim. Seeking advice, I talked to Mel, the farmer who sold me hay and at one time or another had raised the entire contents of Noah's Ark. Mel once said that shooting coyotes was the most fun you could have with your clothes on. He offered advice.

"Don't get goats."

"Why?"

"They'll get their heads stuck in that fence wire of yours."

"Aww, c'mon, they're not that stupid."

"Don't believe it! Even the kids have those bud horns on top of their heads. Just like the barb on a fishing hook. They try to back out and they can't, so they start to bleat. You go rescue them, you give 'em a kick up the arse and go back to what you're doin'. The next thing you know they've done it again. A goat's only interested in what's on the other side of the fence. Have I convinced you yet?"

"I'd still like to get rid of all those brambles and I don't want to spray any herbicides."

"Look, they stink unbelievably, especially the bucks because they piss all over themselves. And the only market is for their meat, unless you get milking goats, in which case you're completely crazy and I'll have nothing more to do with you. And you can only sell the meat to East Indians and then only if it's really lean — no fat at all. You'd be better off starving one of your sheep and shearing it and selling it as a goat."

"Christine likes goat cheese, though."

"Find somebody to sell you the milk then, but don't get goats!"

Obviously Mel was a bit biased, and although I could have sought other opinions, I left the bramble patch where it was and called it wildlife habitat or "unimproved pasture."

>-¦-‹›-•-O-•-‹›-¦-‹

The flat rectangle of land behind the house awaited transformation, all we needed to make our dreams come true was a huge sum of money that, unfortunately, we had neglected either to earn or inherit. But for that, we could plant anything we wanted.

It did have what the Japanese refer to as a "shared landscape," meaning you could see *other people's* well-groomed properties from it. This included a couple of magnificent trees, with cows lounging in the shade, a woodlot with vibrant autumn colours, the even rows of a vineyard and, jutting above the low hills, the peaks of a mountain range (on days when the smog plume from the metropolis didn't obscure it). But the area was sloppy and wet underfoot except in high summer. The rain and snow that fell on the vineyard worked its way downhill toward us, pausing only to nourish Chuck and Angela's well-drained pasture before collecting behind our house in a fetid swamp. I was reminded, too late, of the Boy Scout adage that you don't pitch your tent at the bottom of a hill.

Frogs croaked and mosquitoes multiplied in the puddles between the reeds. There were ducks in the wet season, paddling around in the puddles, but you couldn't put sheep there for fear they'd get hoof rot and there was nothing good to eat in the collection of reeds and sour grasses. It may have been a model wetland to an urban-based environmentalist, but it was a useless piece of wasteland to us, reminiscent of the marshes in English novels (all of which oddly feature characters who die of consumption).

It was easy to see why the water stayed on the surface until the summer sun finally evaporated it: if you dug a hole, the shovel rapidly penetrated the two feet of topsoil and then hit a layer of hardpan clay.

Eventually, we decided to drain the field into the lowest area and create a pond. The hardpan was impervious, so if we dug the pond deep enough it wouldn't dry out in the summer and, if we put in an overflow drain that emptied into a ditch and connected to the township's culvert at the roadside, we wouldn't get flooded in the rainy season. It would be a classic retention pond, the kind serious farmers dig to water livestock or, perhaps, a hay or alfalfa crop in the summer.

And so one spring we engaged Ed, the local excavator, who dug an enormous hole in the back field, banked the soil to provide a modest viewpoint where we could sit for our evening gin and tonic, and dug trenches for drainpipes that fed runoff from the fields into the hole. The hole quickly became a pond and, although it looked alarmingly like a water hazard on a new golf course, we were very pleased.

But what was it to be, other than a water tank? Was it a practical pond to provide irrigation, or merely decorative, a "feature" of our formerly featureless field? It was a quarter acre and 10 feet deep. Maybe we could stock it with trout?

"Do you call it a pond or a lake?" a friend asked.

"I call it an *étang*," Christine replied, harkening back to a trip we had made some years before, when we were impressionable, to Claude Monet's garden at Giverny. Part of that garden is an *étang*, a pond, with the famous water lilies decorating its surface. We were so struck by its beauty — the limpid water reflecting passing clouds and overhanging trees — that we ignored the story of how Monet, by that time a rich artist, had hired half the locals for a few sous a day to divert a channel of the stream into his pond. He then spent a fortune on exotic plants and trees his staff planted for him while he entertained visitors, painted at his easel, drank wine and puffed on Gauloises beneath a large striped parasol. Impetuously, we thought we too could do what Monet had accomplished.

Strong of back and weak of mind, we inaugurated the pond garden on the Queen's birthday with the planting of a liquidambar tree, chosen for its fine fall colour. Its rootball weighed about as much as Christine and I did so we damn near blew a gasket getting it into a wheelbarrow, pushing it over the bumpy ground to the high spot where the gin-and-tonic chairs were and establishing it in the fresh ground. A ceremonial gin and tonic followed while we surveyed the pond: some water lilies here, some water irises along the bank, a couple of expensive trees to block the view of Chuck's sheds along the back — that would be a start.

Other than the fact that the pond bottom was muddy, it was a pleasure to wade in the cool water and I soon decided it could also be a swimmin' hole. However, as its banks were so naked, it was difficult to get naked ourselves without attracting the attention of neighbours who would have a clear view, albeit from a couple of hundred yards away. Nevertheless I soon mastered the art of disrobing on the bank and sliding into the clear water, sometimes joined by my spouse, in a world of utterly delicious privacy. As I paddled slowly along, barn swallows swooped past, skimming low like skipping rocks and dipping their breasts and beaks in the cool water. Dragonflies hovered, curious. This scene could only improve.

In a cold snap that winter, I found my old skates and a sturdy rope and, with Christine on the bank prepared to heave me a lifeline, I zoomed around, stumbling only on the icy ridges where the wind had rippled the freezing water. It took a sickening crack, when I skated across the middle, to send me hastily to the shore.

By the following spring it had become evident that others were at work on the pond garden as well. Some expensive water lilies were devoured by a passing Canada goose. A few shrubs painstakingly planted along the bank were engulfed and snuffed out by the native reeds and grasses reclaiming their habitat. The bullfrogs, once common in the swamp, came back from their holidays and took up residence around the edge, then sent word to friends and relatives who soon trucked across the fields, carrying their suitcases. They were loudest in March when they first awoke from hibernation, celebrating the arrival of spring with a racket audible through the double glazing. Their summer-night serenades were louder than car alarms and during the day the males boomed a mating call like a *thump* on a big bass drum, or a one-note foghorn in a busy harbour.

We were amused by our own conceit. After all, a middle-aged couple of modest means and muscle had presumed to wrestle Mother Nature to the ground. Our adversary was recolonizing the place at an astonishing rate. By the time autumn came around again the pond edge was dotted with cottonwood saplings, their seeds having blown in like a springtime snowfall. I don't know where the willows came from. Migrating ducks flew in and overnighted on the pond. They flapped about and dabbled in the shallows, harvesting the weeds along the edges and in the water, devouring the marsh marigolds we had carefully planted. In the mud on their feet they brought other seeds, including bullrushes that began to grow and spread until stopped by the deep water. We added some pussy willows along one side, a couple of mountain ashes and cut out anything that promised to block interesting sight lines.

Christine, however, was determined to get revenge on the Canada goose that ate her water lily bulbs. Although this might seem irrational, and perhaps was motivated by her Australian heritage, it was in fact a sensible attitude, for Canada geese were an out-of-control population problem in all the parks and farmers' fields around the edge of the city. Neither of us wanted them to colonize the pond, as they would strip it and the nearby fields and drive away the ducks, which we found worthy of our hospitality. Christine was the more motivated and, for a time, was successful at scaring off any geese on the pond by whacking a bamboo pole on the water surface, shouting and leaping around.

But still they came and she began to worry that the neighbours would feel she was uptight, which on the matter of geese she definitely was. She changed tactics and constructed a scarecrow, which looked scary to us but provoked only mild curiosity among the bird population. Doubtless, she should have done a scaregoose. Then, one spring day when she'd been out stomping around, she saw Angela and made a detour to the back fence to catch up on the latest. "Chuck just loves Canada geese," she said. "He feeds them." Angela didn't make it clear whether Chuck also went out at night and harvested one or two.

Trying to be supportive, I joined in the bamboo-pole waving and chasing, but the geese were as determined to stay as we were to move them on. It seemed time to escalate the level of warfare, so I loaded up the pellet gun and marched out to the pond. Now, a pellet gun like the unsophisticated one I'd bought to shoot rats in the barn is not a powerful firearm and once the pellet gets farther than 50 feet from the gun it's got about the same velocity as a shuttlecock. The geese honked warily and stared back at me with their black, beady eyes.

I aimed at the first target, at its thickly feathered body, intending only to whack it to move it along, to show it who was boss. The geese scrambled, airborne, honking wildly. But, to my dismay, the one I'd hit landed rather heavily and ran along the ground, following the flight path of the others as far as it could. I'd maimed it. It stood there, holding one wing out from its body and glaring back at me, hissing. Vowing never to use the gun again, I stomped back to the house and looked for a nature program to watch on TV.

Now we had a wounded goose, resident on the pond and determined to get his revenge. As he was apparently going to be around for a while, I named him Mr. Walker and I was able to report daily on his activities. A flock of passing geese saw Mr. Walker and decided he needed company, so now there were 20 geese on the pond. Within a week Mr. Walker was grazing on the field, accompanied by 50 caregivers. After a month or so, his wing healed and he flew away, taking his friends with him.

A call to the wildlife people ensued: "Don't let them raise goslings next spring," they said. "Addle the eggs. Just give 'em a good shake. The Canada goose population is out of control and addling's the best way to deal with it. Don't break the eggs, because they'll just start another nest. Don't shoot the goose with a pellet gun."

So we prowled around the edges and ditches and everywhere we found a nest we gave the eggs a good shake. Sometimes I had to stand guard with a pole to keep the gander from nailing us. There was a whole lotta shakin' goin' on. Eventually we got the goose population down to two, which made life a little easier for the smaller birds around the pond. Even Chuck appeared to lose interest in them.

Meanwhile, the hayloft of our barn had begun to be colonized by pigeons, the one creature I would turn back at the gangplank to my ark: defiler of the great monuments of Europe, the winged rat of the world's cities (as Canada geese are the winged pig and squirrels the tree rat). I was afraid they would eventually drive out the barn owl, a rare and fine creature, although sometimes if the pickings were a bit slim in the fields, the owl would kill a pigeon and leave the scraps for the rats and the chickens. From time to time I'd sneak up the stairs to the hayloft and take a shot at the pigeons cooing (and crapping) along the metal rail that ran below the ridge of the roof. Occasionally I'd get one, but more often they'd just panic and flap away. One day, though, I nailed a rather pretty pigeon that looked more like a dove.

A couple of days later, when I was working out in the back field, Chuck rode by on his horse and stopped to chat.

"You know my homin' pigeons?" he began.

"I didn't know you had pigeons."

"Just love 'em. They fly in a tight little flock around my place. I'm thinking of racing them in the fall."

"Oh, so that's what they are," I muttered. I tried to keep my face averted, afraid I was beginning to look guilty.

"Keep an eye out for them, will you?" he asked. "I'm missing a couple."

I recalled watching a very fast hawk knock something out of the sky, but it was too far away to see the identity of the victim.

"Sure, I'll do that, Chuck," I said, trying not to stammer.

In the winter, with the pond level as high as it could go and the grasses dead and flat, we sat at the back window of the house and watched the migrating birds. With a copy of *The Boys' Book of Waterfowl* in one hand and the binoculars in the other, I was able to identify a number of unusual ducks, some of which made little more than a pit stop. Others stayed for a week or two, sharing the pond and its weedy edges with the usual throng of mallards before moving on. There were widgeons with their low, whistling calls, pintails and teals, ring-necked ducks with banded feathering, common mergansers with swept-back haircuts, hooded mergansers with grotesquely large, black-edged crests and black-and-white buffleheads, small diving ducks that would disappear below the surface and emerge many seconds later on the other side of the pond. When the buffleheads wanted to take off, they had to run across the surface of the water to get enough speed. Hawks and eagles circled high above, usually content with feasts of field mice, but always on the lookout for any sick or wounded bird that would make an easy meal. One spring day there was even a trumpeter swan that stopped for a few hours to refuel before flying north.

All along the edges of the pond, in the willows and the bullrushes, songbirds made their nests. Hummingbirds nested in the shrubs in Christine's garden and divided their time between the garden flowers and a feeder we hung from the pergola above the front terrace. The males, with their iridescent vermilion breasts, performed astonishing courtship rituals, usually involving a series of vertical dives and flights so high that they almost disappeared against the sky.

True to their names, the barn swallows occupied every nook and cranny in the barn, building their deep mud-and-straw nests along the ceiling joists above the byre, anchoring them to any ridge or light fixture. Their enemies were crows that systematically tried to rob the nests of eggs and, later, of baby birds, which they washed in the sheep's water tank (the sheep, being vegans, disapproved). Whenever I could find both my glasses and the gun, I shot a crow and hung it up in the entranceway to the barn — a warning that was usually heeded, crows being the least bird-brained of all the winged creatures. During the evening, in the huge pool of air between the barn, the house and the pond, dozens of swallows dived and swooped like a reenactment of the Battle of Britain, harvesting insects by the mouthful and delivering them to the nests. The four or five babies in each nest lined up with their heads sticking out and chorused when their mother — only *their* mother — approached at a speed only slightly below that of sound. On the floor below, lurking among the hay bales and grain barrels, the cat waited to scoop up any unlucky baby that reached too far and tumbled out.

One swallow, probably tired of the traffic congestion, found a spot at the back of the house and built a nest atop a halogen light fixture that was intended to illuminate the barbecue when I was out late in the evening reducing a piece of lamb or chicken to cinders. By the time I noticed the nest it was already completed and home to several eggs, so I left it, even though I was a bit annoyed. At the end of the season, once all the swallows had flown south, I removed the nest and enclosed the light fixture with chicken wire to discourage a repeat performance.

The following spring, when the swallow returned, she evidently was pleased with the wire, as it made it easier to attach a new nest.

It was astonishing how fast the native trees and shrubs grew around the pond. The liquidambar, which when we planted it dominated the landscape, was quickly dwarfed by wind-borne seedlings that shot up to 25 feet. With only a little push from us, a piece of rich natural habitat had emerged in our former swamp. Every evening in the summer and fall when the weather was fair we sat and watched the passing parade of birds and frogs. The light on the pastures and trees turned golden as the sun sank toward the treetops, deepening the reflections of bullrushes and sleeping ducks in the barely rippled water. Mallards found the pond a safe place to pass the few flightless weeks while they moulted; the males, usually so dramatic with their bright-green heads, became a dull, dun-coloured brown, quite different from the mottled, brindle-coloured females who lose their bright-blue wing flash. Occasionally a few more mallards would arrive, oblivious to us, coming in low and fast, dropping their wings like airplane flaps and lowering their landing gear until, at the last minute, they pulled their wings back and levelled out, stretching their webbed feet ahead of them and skiing in. Watching them land, and contemplating the arabesques of the swallows, I would have traded my remaining years for a few seasons as a bird.

As the afternoon breeze dropped and the temperature began to cool with the onset of evening, the sheep rose from the cud-chewing, sociable torpor in which they'd spent the heat of the day and returned to grazing. Sometimes a killdeer waded along the edge of the pond, or a goldfinch or red-winged blackbird swayed on a bullrush, or fluttered high up into the blue as if only to take in the view. The bullfrogs lurked silently, their pop-up eyes and yellow heads just breaking the pond's calm surface.

Reluctantly we would get up from our chairs, moving slowly so as not to disturb any of the pond's residents, and walk quietly back toward the house, nodding to the sheep as we passed.

Every spring in the thick, reedy grass around the edge of the pond, mallards hatched their eggs and then tried to raise the ducklings. One evening when we were enthroned on our chairs, a mallard hen motored slowly around the curve in the pond with nine ducklings in her wake. The following evening there were six. Then, to our dismay, there was only one, *all by itself*, the mother having fled in frustration, I suppose. It tooled around in the open water, letting out a plaintive, lonely whistle, far from any reach or help we could give it. The following day it was gone. It seemed likely that the bullfrogs were the culprits, although maybe the barn cat, the owl or a hawk had a tooth or talon in it too. Thereafter, we cheered on a heron that made regular visits to the pond and hunted in its stealthy, stately way, with its rapier beak so lightning-quick to spear any inattentive frog.

On a desperately hot summer day I decided to take a dip, even though the surface was quite thickly covered in algae. Waving green weeds beckoned me like mermaids from below. "You'll be sorry," warned the sensible Christine as I plunged in and splashed around, taking care to keep my teeth together to avoid ingesting slime. In the middle of the pond the water was almost clear, and deliciously cool. Eventually I struggled out and up the bank to dry off in the hot sun, before dressing and walking back to the house. I'd planned to hose myself off, but I was distracted by the need to move some portable fencing and then by something else. After a typically meandering farm afternoon, I finally had a shower.

The following morning I was covered in itchy red bumps. *Yer gonna need an ocean, of calamine lotion.*

It took a couple of days for the itch to go away. As I had no intention of going back into the pond I thought no more about it until one day I was listening to the radio and an on-air guest from the government wildlife service described an outbreak of "swimmer's itch" on all the freshwater lakes. It was caused by a tiny snail — a parasite — on ducks. The antidote was to hose yourself off as soon as you got out of the water.

With that bit of information under my belt, as it were, I waded back into the pond to harvest some of the weeds. After a while spent pitchforking clumps of them onto the bank, where Christine scooped them up and put them in a wheelbarrow, I emerged onto the dry land. Christine stared at me in horror.

"You've got a leech on your leg!" she screamed.

I can't remember what happened next. Did she run away mumbling "Yuk! Disgusting! Horrible!"? Did I try to pry it off? It did eventually release its grip and plopped back into the pond, considerably larger. That was the final straw. The pond would have to look after itself.

We turned our attention to the ROWBOATS FOR SALE section in the local newspaper.

We inherited with the farm a small tabby barn cat that was as untamed as any of the creatures in the hedges. The previous owners had named her Gretchen. They had managed to trap her and get her fixed at Willem's neutering emporium down the road: a smart move, as a kitty in heat summons every tom for miles around. Feral cats are curious creatures, secretive and shy. They survive on the edge of rural civilization like the homeless living in the nooks and crannies of big cities. Compared with wild dogs (often crossbreeds known locally as "coydogs") that run in packs and are aggressive, predatory and dangerous, feral cats are loners, seeking each other out only for one-night stands.

When we first moved to the farm — between cats ourselves, Smedley having been hit by a car in the city — everywhere we turned we kept glimpsing a black-and-white cat, patterned like a Holstein cow. As it kept changing size, we soon realized there was more than one. Occasionally they sprayed the side of the white barn. All were sniffly, with weepy eyes. I did my best to make the barn unwelcome to them in order to avoid the chore of kitten-drowning.

We found the Holstein-cat mother lode on a summer's day not long after a sign had gone up on the corner, advertising freshly dug potatoes and pointing toward the end of the road. We investigated and found another, smaller sign nailed to the post that supported the mailbox and pointing up the driveway. A few yards along, a third sign said HONK FOR POTATOES. Unfortunately we were on foot, but a farmer-type in overalls with sweaty, flattened hair from prolonged hat-wearing was exiting one of the sheds and spotted us. He came over to the gate. Taking minimal risk, conversationally speaking, he asked: "Y'here for potatoes?"

Receiving an affirmative answer, he beckoned us to follow him to a low shed with galvanized tin siding and roof. In the gloom we could see mounds of potatoes and, moving around in the shadows, at least four of the Holstein cats.

"So this is where they're from!" I exclaimed.

"Whuh? The potatoes?"

"No, the cats. We've got a few down at our place, always hanging around in the barn."

"Yeah, they're everywhere," he said indifferently. "One of 'em just had kittens the other day."

Christine and I looked at each other. Seeking to change the subject, she inquired, "I guess you have to rotate your crops regularly."

"Yup. Some years I grow red ones and other years white ones."

He seemed unwilling to offer any further insights into his business, so we bought a bag of the white ones, thanked him, and lugged them home. A year or so later, by which time we were growing our own potatoes, he had moved on; the new people, who saw the property more as a rural estate than a working farm, demolished the sheds, seeded the potato fields with grass and brought in horses. Gradually the Holstein cats disappeared from the neighbourhood, helped along, no doubt, by the coyotes.

Gretchen survived all such invasions of the barn, keeping to herself, somehow trusting that her place was secure and we would fight her turf battles for her. She was truly wary of us and would vanish like morning mist over the pastures if we came anywhere near her. Gretchen was as clean and neat as a cat could be, with a shiny brown-striped coat and white stockings. She never appeared matted and dishevelled, no matter how bad the weather became in the winter. Although she was around our barn much of the time, it was possible she spent her absences in a neighbour's barn rather than hunting and sleeping in the hedges. A time-share cat?

She lived on longer than any cat I ever had in the city, where traffic eventually claimed them all. A patient hunter, Gretchen roamed the fields day and night and could sometimes be spotted sitting motionless in the tall grass, or walking along the top rail of one of the fences, looking down into the grass and imagining she was an eagle. In the mornings, when I went down to the barn to fill a bucket with grain for the chickens, I would often see her half asleep in the hay bales in a strategic spot that gave her command over the doorway and an escape route into the hayloft above.

The previous owners had always left a bowl of cat food out for her, but who knew whether she got any of it. There were certainly other cats, such as the Holsteins, that cruised through for a feeding, plus rats, an occasional dangerous raccoon and a whole slew of possums.

The possums were the kind that look like a cross between a pig and a rat and are so slow-moving that they're the most common roadkill in our part of the country. A possum is rarely awesome. Although they did no real damage, if given the opportunity they'd have eaten the chicken eggs and would eventually have taken over the place, so I began trapping them and taking them down to the park. In one spell, over Christmas, I trapped a possum a day, drove it to the park, shook out the cage and told the animal in a stern voice never to come back. I could have been the Humane Society's poster boy.

Gretchen gradually got used to our presence and no longer fled, preferring to hover in the shadows. For her loyalty, we put out a little dry cat food in a bowl on a high shelf where the hens wouldn't find it. (Although one hen did, learning to fly up, push Gretchen back, and peck up all the goodies. She was rewarded by being turned into soup; let *that* be a lesson to anyone who is smarter than average.) Eventually Gretchen became tame enough to jump up onto the shelf while I put the cat food in the bowl, but if I made a noise or any sudden movement she would leap instantly up the wall and disappear into the hayloft. If I moved slowly and spoke in a low voice she would purr softly and, on a good day, tentatively put out a paw with the claws sheathed and pat the back of my kibble-filled hand.

Barn cats normally don't last too long, even if they manage to avoid bigger and faster predators. Their main diet is chubby field mice — voles. According to a pamphlet at Willem's, vole is the perfect food for cats. Unfortunately, though, voles are the intermediate host for intestinal worms and have tough bones that eventually break cats' teeth. A wormy cat with bad teeth will starve or quickly get taken out by a stronger predator. In nature, nothing dies of old age. Every few months, Christine would pop a worm pill into some tinned food and stand by to make sure Gretchen swallowed it.

Obviously we were making progress toward taming her, but I was unsure to what end. A friend who visited one day asked why we didn't befriend her and bring her inside. But then what would we do for a barn cat? She (Gretchen, not the friend) played a useful role. However, as the years rolled by it became evident that her lifestyle was taking its toll; she always seemed hungry and was having difficulty chewing the dry cat food, sometimes gulping it down whole. One spring, when the voles were running hot and thick and she ought to have been as sleek as a panther, her coat looked dry and scruffy and she had lost a lot of weight. We decided to try to tame her, using tinned mystery-meat cat food in case she got so weak and frail that she had to be hauled off to Willem's funeral parlour or brought inside for comfort and a dignified death.

In response to the tinned food, she began to show up religiously at six o'clock in the evening, when the poultry gathered expectantly in front of the barn for their before-bed snack. For the first few days she stood back and watched, keeping her distance as before, but the smell was too much and soon she was right up at the can, sniffing and purring impatiently as I struggled with the pull tab. Once she got her snout into the food, I tried stroking her back. She flinched but didn't move away and kept purring. I stroked more and she purred louder. When I touched her ear she looked up sharply, with an expression that said, "Watch it, Buster!"

Alas, her tolerance was only a rural version of cupboard love.

The Duck Tapes

I've never been successful with ducks, so should have just been content to share the farm with the wild ones on the pond. Hobby farmer's report card: Sheep, B+; Chickens, B-; Barn Cat, A; Ducks, D.

During the first spring on the farm, in a Noah-like mood, we went to buy a pair of geese and at the same time picked up a pair of Muscovy ducks. Shopping trips are so often like that — you go with the intention of buying just one thing, yet come home with a carload. You also have to keep in mind when you go out to somebody's roadside poultry farm, beckoned by a hand-lettered sign on the gate offering DUCK'S 4 SAIL, that there will be no "satisfaction or money cheerfully refunded" statement on the invoice, if there happens to be an invoice. You're on your own. Fortunately you're not looking at major bucks to bring home the ducks — $5 to $10 each — especially if you want only garden-variety ducks to eat slugs and trim and fertilize the grass.

Except when they're young, Muscovy ducks are ugly-looking things. We bought ours young. When we were halfway home, Christine began to mutter: "Muscovies ... Muscovies ... aren't they the ones with the weird growth on their faces?" She was correct. When Muscovy ducks mature they develop a carbuncle atop their beaks. However, we did recall hearing that they were good egg-layers and mothers, though we were more than a little vague about other characteristics. Like most farm ducks, they would have heavy bodies and short wings, allowing them to waddle and swim, but limiting their flying ability to that of an overloaded airplane.

One of the ducks lasted only a week. Old friends from the city out for a Sunday drive in the country dropped by unexpectedly to see our new place. We found a flagon of wine and they stayed through the afternoon. Eventually Christine pulled out a brochure for a pizza place. Surprised (and slightly disconcerted) that we were *that* close to modern conveniences, we decided to give it a try. "It'll be 45 minutes," the receptionist said. Taking him at his word, I staggered down to open the gate at the appointed time. Half an hour later the delivery boy chugged up the driveway with the lukewarm pizza. The evening passed pleasantly enough, but when our visitors left I realized the gate had been open the whole time. The next morning I followed a trail of white feathers and found one of the ducks, lightly chewed but not eaten, indicating that a passing dog was probably the culprit. A well-fed dog, a pet, killing for pleasure. All things being equal, it was a relatively cheap lesson in gate management.

Chastened by the experience, I resolved to ensure a long life for Muscovy number 2, who became known as Ducky Daddles after the character in the Chicken Little story. For a time she contentedly waddled around in the barnyard with the geese and our growing flock of chickens. However, I was surprised one morning to see her out on the pond, which was separated from the barnyard by a line of wire fence and 50 yards of pasture. Perhaps she had sensed the proximity of water and had squeezed through the fence? Although safe on the pond, she was a sitting duck, as it were, while waddling to and from the barnyard. Even a myopic coyote could spot her gleaming white plumage on the pond, like a neon sign flashing DINER on a lonesome highway. When she was grazing in the pasture, I grabbed a long pole and, with the intention of herding her back toward the barn, got between her and the pond.

We were making good progress until she suddenly decided

to do an end run around me and head back to the pond. I loped across the rough ground, cutting off her route, but she doubled back like a skilful football player avoiding a tackle. I cut her off again. She broke into a waddling run, but I was gaining on her. Then she unfurled her wings, gave a mighty flap and was airborne, flying just above the ground. She'll tire, I puffed, but instead she flew up into the sky effortlessly, made a graceful arc around the pond and headed back toward the house. By the time I'd limped back in, she'd landed on a fence and was gazing back at me with a defiant expression.

As I approached she stood up fully, stretched her wings flapped, then exposed herself... no, *himself* — a pink corkscrew emerged through the white feathers, glinted briefly in the sun, then retracted. Ducky Daddles was a boy! We bonded instantly.

When I came out of the house the next morning to hand out the grain, he was waiting for me, sitting on the fence just outside the mudroom door. Late in the afternoon he flew in from the pond, sometimes circling the house towing an imaginary banner that read HUNGRY! He then flew down to join the throng of poultry waiting for me at the barn.

But, as I said, I've never been successful with ducks, and one morning when I emerged he wasn't there. After feeding the chickens and geese I went looking for him, and found him in the field. He was on his back with his chest ripped open and his heart torn out, as if killed by a Satanist. Assigning feelings to the attacker, I asked Christine, "What kind of creature would do that to another?"

Needless to say, this whodunit was featured on America's Most Wanted — the Farm Channel version. We also discussed the case with friends and neighbours when prompted by a question such as, "How are those animals of yours doing?" But no one had a clue who the culprit might be.

One afternoon a small, rusty car pulled up to the gate and a young man walked up the driveway. He was a biology student from the university, he said, completing his doctoral thesis on owls.

"I'm driving around looking for old barns like yours. Have you got an owl in there?" he asked.

"Definitely. We see her flying at night, or hear her if we're in the barn."

"Can I gather some pellets? Part of my thesis is on owl diets." Pellets are an owl's version of a hair ball, black turds about the size of a small sausage, containing mashed-up fur and bones and other indigestible glop.

"Sure," I said, "and come in for coffee afterward."

He joined us later and talked for a while about his vocation.

"They're on the 'vulnerable' list now," he told us. "Barn owls aren't endangered yet, but they're losing habitat as old barns like yours get demolished." Our barn had a tall, second-storey hayloft that, in the days before mechanized balers, stored a huge volume of loose hay for winter feed. Using plans from an owl site on the Internet, we had built a plywood nesting box and attached it high on the barn's back wall.

"When the horse people build barns," I said, gesturing in the direction of the riding stable across the street, "they build low-pitched roofs using trusses, so there's no space left for the owls to nest."

"Even cattle ranchers aren't keeping their old barns," he said. "They use those round, plastic-wrapped bales now and store them outdoors." Like huge marshmallows weighing a half ton, plastic-wrapped hay bales were a recent addition to the country landscape.

I asked him what barn owls ate.

"They usually eat voles, but occasionally they'll kill something bigger."

"Like a duck?"

"Sure, but it's very characteristic of predatory birds, including owls, that they eat the heart first. They prefer the rest once it breaks down into carrion."

Not long afterward, feeling feckless and duckless, we picked up a fresh pair from our neighbours down the road. These were not Muscovies. Joyce was a Cayuga, a breed of duck originally from Lake Cayuga, New York. She had a long, elegant body and glossy black feathers with an iridescent viridian sheen. Equally distinguished in shape and movement, Bill was a Khaki Campbell, brown and green, looking like a tall Englishman in a Harris tweed jacket. In the water, they swam with their breasts deep and their tail feathers held high, graceful as sailing yachts when compared to the wild ducks that move around like tugboats. But Bill didn't last long either. He was killed by a coyote and was replaced by a young, Khaki Campbell named Bruce, who had even sleeker, matinée-idol looks. Joyce sashayed alluringly around the pond, making all the wild ducks wilder and forcing her mate to fight off the good-for-nothing drifters.

In response to the death of Bill and sundry other raids by Mother Nature's predators, I had improved the outside fences to the point where I no longer felt the need to lock up the geese at night. Fort Goose, the enclosure I'd built for that purpose, thus stood vacant with its door open, awaiting a new use. In the spring, when it became apparent that Joyce was looking for a place to nest, I put some old hay under a tipped-up wooden box in the corner and enticed her in with a handful of grain. The ruse worked, and she had soon arranged the hay into a beautiful round nest lined with her own down, into which she deposited an egg a day. After each addition, she'd scatter more hay, nonchalantly, behaving like someone who whistles to distract you from what they're doing. With Bruce following, she'd waddle back to the pond to resume her grazing, dabbling and paddling.

Joyce was one smart duck and Bruce — like many husbands — knew enough to follow her lead. She had a remarkable sense of direction (after all, wild ducks migrate), certainly compared with the geese and the chickens, who could quite easily get trapped behind something no bigger than a fire screen and be unable to figure out how to get around it. If a chicken could see where it wanted to go it would head straight for it, even if it meant walking smack into a wire fence, whereas Joyce could reason her way through a maze. Like the chickens, many of the sheep had little sense of direction, unable to comprehend that you sometimes have to start a journey by taking a few steps in the wrong direction. It was a good thing they had Mary, who took a more Zen approach, to lead them.

After she had laid about a dozen eggs, Joyce began to sit them and I put a mark on the calendar 30 days hence for the hatch. I kept the Fort Goose door open so she could come and go if she wanted a snack or a quick splash. The plan was to lock her and Bruce in once the ducklings hatched, to be sure none of them were attacked by the geese or a cat. As the hatching date approached, I dug a hole for the large watering bowl the sheep used during the winter.

While we waited, all of our country friends and neighbours told us duck stories. Traditional farms often kept a duck to sit eggs, even chicken eggs, but you had to be careful that the mother duck didn't march newly hatched chicks into a pond with her or they'd drown. If you sat a broody hen on duck eggs you had to keep the ducklings away from water, because the oil gland in their mouth that waterproofs their feathers doesn't develop until they're fledged. Mother ducks groom their newly hatched ducklings, so that they're buoyant right away. Hearing all this, our confidence in Joyce's mothering abilities grew — she was such a purposeful, down-to-business, matter-of-fact duck, we were sure she had all the angles covered.

This was fortunate, as the duckling hatching was going to coincide with a long-planned vacation. On a neighbour's recommendation, we contacted a potential farm-sitter by the name of Charmaine, a young woman who was a barmaid in the local pub. She'd be used to looking after animals. According to our neighbour, she owned a thoroughbred horse that took so much of her income she was forced to live with her divorced mother in a trailer park on the edge of town. Putting two and two together, we surmised that this was why she was so willing to house-sit.

Joyce had not budged for a couple of days and hissed loudly whenever I went near her, so I put some food down and closed the Fort Goose door. On the day that Charmaine came over to confirm arrangements and pick up the key, Joyce got up from her nest and, leaving a rubble of broken shells behind, waddled over to the pond with eight beautiful ducklings in tow. Bruce stayed at a distance, but quacked encouragement. The ducklings set a new standard for cuteness on the farm. They were little balls of grey fluff, with bright, black, beady eyes, oversized webbed feet, and bills that looked as if they were made of black rubber. They began to forage through the grass for seeds and bugs, snap at flies and shovel up the mix of crushed grain I'd scattered. In the pond, they bobbed about like the toy ducks in my childhood bathtub. The proud parents quacked happily and Joyce tucked the ducklings under her wings all night to keep them warm.

The next day we were off, leaving Charmaine in the saddle. It was summer and there wasn't a whole lot for her to do — just check the waterers for the sheep and chickens and scatter a little grain around in the morning. We hardly gave the place another thought until we returned several days later. As we came up the driveway, there was the usual complement of chickens scratching and pecking under the poplar trees in the driveway, the sheep off in the distance. As we carried our stuff into the house, the first thing I saw was a note from Charmaine: "Call me about the ducks."

At first we could see nothing amiss. Bruce sat quietly in the grass and quacked a little, while Joyce worked through the long grass with her babies. One, two, three ... a fourth — that was all. Only four! I went back to the house and called Charmaine, who was just getting ready to go to the pub for her evening shift.

"I feel awful," she began. "Every morning I went down, there was another one dead."

"How come?"

"Drowned ... in the little pond ... all the same. I couldn't figure it out."

Puzzled, Christine and I went back to Fort Goose to inspect the family.

The sound of the geese honking and chattering suddenly triggered a distant memory.

"Do you remember reading an article or hearing somebody say that a gander will kill his own goslings if given half a chance?" I asked Christine. "Maybe it's the same for ducks."

"It certainly isn't for chickens," she said, "but it's a thought."

Thinking Bruce might be the culprit, so we herded him out. He was really annoyed, quacking and pushing against the wire mesh to get back in. Joyce quacked at him for a minute, but soon went back to her mothering.

The following day, the local paper carried the story:

RURAL DAD KILLS 4
Grief counsellors dispatched

We got a call from Jan. "I saw the story in the *Advance*," he said. "Sorry to hear about that."

"Have you ever seen it happen before?" I asked him.

"Well, I've never had ducks. But I remember when I was a boy in Holland, one year when it was really cold and the food supplies were low, wild male ducks on the canals were drowning others. Guess it's just nature."

"There've been no further drownings since we banished him. He must have been the guilty party."

It was most curious that the four survivors were boys. We accepted Bruce's plea of temporary insanity and, once his remaining offspring had grown and fledged, we reunited them. For the balance of the summer, and through the fall and the winter, I didn't pay them much attention, being busy elsewhere with the round of seasonal farm chores, putting to the back of my mind my inability to manage waterfowl.

Soon, *five* males began to make life miserable for Joyce and, by association, for us. I had no problem with the antics of the wild things on the pond, but we demanded a certain level of decorum from all of our animals in the barnyard.

"If you want to behave like that," I lectured them, "move to the big city where it's more acceptable."

To make matters worse, Killer Dad, aka Bruce, developed a sore leg and, reduced to hopping and limping, could not assert dominance over his sons. Two of them were determined to avenge the death of their siblings and began attacking Bruce, beaking him about the neck and face and stomping on him. On a few occasions, I managed to separate them, as did Arthur the rooster, who would leap into the fray. Even Jethro the gander, who couldn't stand any commotion of which he wasn't the cause, ran right over them in his excitement. When the two sons also chased their mother it was the last straw, so I took them to the auction, where they commanded $12 each! The barnyard returned to something approaching a state of calm.

However, Bruce's leg didn't get any better and we felt we had to seek medical advice. He was worth the investment, as we were by nature liberals, believers in the inherent goodness of ducks and willing to give him a second chance. I made an appointment for him at Willem's animal repair clinic.

"Now, we only have you down here for a lamb named Loretti," said the receptionist. "How is she, by the way?"

"Oh, fine, but we may barbecue her later this year."

"And this Bruce, he's a ... ?"

"Duck. Do you want the breed? He's a Khaki Campbell."

"No, we don't have a place on the form for that level of detail."

With his gammy leg, Bruce was easy to catch and, wrapped in an old towel on Christine's lap, he rode in style to the hospital. Willem was on time and told us to go into his examining room, where an assistant was just wiping off and disinfecting the stainless steel table. I put Bruce down and held him lightly with thumb and finger around his neck.

"We don't get too many ducks in here," Willem said as he came into the room.

"And at these prices you won't get many more," I said, reprising the old joke about the kangaroo that hops into the expensive cocktail lounge.

Bruce gave *his* opinion by suddenly and violently shitting in a great, wet splat onto the stainless steel. When we'd got that cleaned up, Willem began to feel the leg, rotating the joint and trying to locate the problem. He looked perplexed.

"It all seems normal," he reported. "Nothing broken, so it's probably a pinched nerve."

"Will it get better?"

"Hard to say, but try to confine him so he can get some rest and improve his diet." He reached up to a shelf and, from among the rolls of duck tape, took down a huge jar with DUCK VITAMINS printed on its label. He scooped some into a smaller jar. "Try to put this on his food or in his water."

Back at the farm, we put Bruce into Fort Goose and herded Joyce in with him, leaving the two remaining sons to keep each other company and consort with the mallards on the pond. But as the weeks went by there was no improvement in Bruce's condition. Joyce became restless and annoyed, having been unable to read the "for better or worse, in sickness and in health" part of the nuptial agreement, and Bruce seemed quite listless. Maybe I should have killed him, but it was hard to kill a duck. They have such agreeable, quacking faces and I didn't think I could whack his head off with a hatchet. I'd have to wring his neck or smother him or something equally unpleasant. Christine and I agreed to do nothing.

In the middle of the summer I had to go away for a few days, leaving Christine alone on the farm. I arrived back elated, thrilled to smell the dairy air after days of hotels and airplanes, but my mood quickly changed when I saw her. She was visibly upset.

"Bruce is dead," she cried. "These things always happen when you're away!"

"What? How?" I said, trying to comfort her.

"The owl ... it ripped his head off and ate the heart, just like Ducky Daddles!" She was in tears. "I had to scoop him up with the shovel, he was such a mess."

"Poor Bruce." Poor Christine.

"He's in a bucket in the barn."

Later that day I dug a big hole in the garden and carefully upended the bucket over it. Bruce's yellow beak was fixed in a smile. That's what makes ducks so hard to treat as anything other than pets — they always seem to be smiling at you. Christine planted the customary rosebush over him.

Joyce scarcely missed a beat. As I said, she was a practical, down-to-earth duck. If human, she would probably have coped well in a war zone. She resumed her routine with her two sons, returning to the pond every night through the winter, showing up at the barn for grain morning and afternoon, inspecting the garden every day for slugs and snails. With the arrival of spring the two sons fought for dominance until Joyce began to build a nest, this time in the shelter of a shrub beside the house. Their rivalry finished for the year, the two sons waddled off together and went back to the pond.

Joyce laid about 10 eggs in a new nest before beginning to sit, puffing herself up and hissing at us if we took too much notice of her. A month later she emerged into the yard with only three ducklings, one of which seemed weak and had a limp. Perhaps it was the inbreeding, or her age, that reduced her hatch. Using a couple of long poles, I herded her and her brood into Fort Goose and closed the door to exclude the two eager fathers.

It quickly became evident that she was abandoning the third duckling, as it wasn't properly groomed and nearly drowned. The two healthy ones were growing quickly and getting all their mother's attention, so we made an executive decision to move the weakling away and try to raise it separately. I had a big cage full of chicks of about the same age — ones I'd hatched in the incubator — into which I put the duckling, but it was pecked to death within a day. The healthy ducklings turned out to be males, as luck would have it.

Little Goose Coop

Of all the animals, the most pet-like were the two geese we bought to stock the ark during our first spring. Initially we thought we were being practical, as we had seen villages and farms in Europe where geese acted as vigilant watchdogs, requiring little training to achieve the obnoxious quality that bored dogs develop only after prolonged neglect by their owners. Dogs in the country can be a great nuisance. If they're left alone too long, they bark themselves silly ("Bark if you love peace and quiet!"); if they're not fenced in, they roam and occasionally form dangerous packs. Pets in the country require *control*, just like livestock.

We were most successful with the animals we'd bought for practical purposes, although the sheep and the chickens would probably disagree with my definition of a "practical purpose." A few of the sheep, notably Eliza and her brother Eddie (during the time he was in our employ), and a few chickens like Arthur, Dave and Patsy Cline, had special status, names and received a higher quality of conversation, although they didn't get invited into the house.

A Black Orpington hen named Favey (because she was my favourite) also became something of a pet. She had a very large body, as shapeless as a sack of coal yet beautifully feathered in black with a turquoise sheen and a tiny red-wattled head. She was placid and slow — I had to be careful I didn't run her over with the tractor. If she were a wild creature, she'd have been roadkill. To be honest, she was only slightly more animated than a pet rock, but she did go broody once or twice and hatched a few chicks. She would always stand patiently and look at me if I wanted to have a talk with her. She outlived all the other hens — mainly because I didn't send her to the auction — although she eventually lost the sight in one eye. In fact, her face swelled up on one side and her comb and wattles lost all their colour. She spent her days staggering around, so I contemplated putting her out of her misery. Seeing her, deflated our city friends. "How gross!" they exclaimed and beat a path back to the house.

Achieving a balance between the pets and the practical live-stock is the biggest challenge when running a small farm. Too practical and the farm becomes like a forced labour camp, which can hardly be justified given the emotional stress (on farmer and animals) and the minuscule profit margin. Too many pets and you have a retirement home, requiring almost as much work as a food-production line.

Your first time buying a goose is most fraught with danger. An unscrupulous goose salesman can easily pass off two boys or two girls as a couple when they're young, before the girl matures and develops the egg sac that almost drags on the ground between her legs. The male stays relatively flat on the bottom, with everything hidden internally. Although we were assured by the woman who sold us the winsome twosome that they were in fact a couple, we *were* from the city....

They were Embdens, snow-white with orange webbed feet, orange saw-toothed beaks and beady, cobalt-blue eyes behind which the skull receded, leaving a space about the size of a pea for the brain. (As a neighbour said about his peacock, "His brain is a nerve with a knot in it.") Their small, comical heads were located at the ends of long, graceful necks, making them above knee height on me. They could be Christmas dinner if they didn't fit in. To allow for the distinct possibility of gender confusion, we gave them unisex names culled from *The English Aristocrat's Baby Name Book*: Hilary and Beverley. Beverley was the big, docile one, probably the girl. Hilary was more aggressive, a little smaller, with a black mark under his right eye.

We got them home and put them into the Little Goose Coop, a former dog kennel surrounded by chain-link fence, beside the shack at the top of the driveway. Seen through the chain link, they had the "junkyard goose" look we needed to protect the place from marauding JDs (Juvenile Delinquents) and JWs. After a couple of days I let them out into the farmyard, where they passed the heat of the day snoozing underneath the pickup truck. Every evening I herded them back into the Little Goose Coop, as I was still uncertain about the quality of our fences.

One evening a few weeks later, we were driving home on a country road when a cop pulled us over.

"Both your taillights are out," he said, writing a ticket. Strange.... The following day I checked the fuses, found them fine, took off the red reflectors and looked at the bulbs, which seemed okay, then crawled underneath to have a look. The wiring was absolutely ripped to pieces. The geese had pulled and tugged at anything exposed until it was shredded. As I put a hastily assembled GMD (Goose Management Device), made of boards, around the back of the truck, I wondered whether this would be their only transgression.

To distract them I pointed in the direction of Christine's garden, where they soon busied themselves ripping out climbing vines and destroying tiny, valuable seedlings. Countering deftly, she showed them my vegetable garden where, in a matter of minutes, they gave some carefully tended romaine lettuce a brush cut. Then some city friends dropped by uninvited for a visit, so I casually let the geese wander over to their shiny car. Enraged by the sight of other geese, they beaked at their reflections until, with the arrival of nighttime, they drove their adversaries away.

Perhaps I've exaggerated, but only slightly. They *were* destructive, at one point ripping all the wiring out of my rototiller, but I must admit they compensated by being watchdogs and amusing us with their behaviour. When they weren't converting grain directly into noise, they ambled around the barnyard, never more than a few paces apart, occasionally honking at a plane or bird passing overhead (especially a Canada goose) or beaking a chicken out of the way, like punks shouldering pedestrians aside on a city sidewalk.

Neighbours, especially the ones with hearing aids, commented on how nice it was to have geese around again. They had their own Mother Goose stories: of the pair of geese a couple of roads over that went for a walk together every day through the gate and down the road; of the little girl who was met every afternoon at the school bus stop by her goose. "Them geese'll last a long time," said the old guy who rode by on his bicycle every day. I liked the way nothing could get up the driveway without our hearing about it. I stopped locking them up at night in the Little Goose Coop after learning that a couple of the commuters farther along the road had had their homes burgled.

And people *were* afraid of the geese. One day, when we had advertised a fridge for sale, a couple of rather suspicious characters called to get the address and came by. One of them looked around so avidly that I thought he was going to wrench his neck. Sensing evil with their goose ESP, Bev and Hilary came up behind him and, with their beaks low and sweeping the ground like cobras, growled menacingly. *Aie-aie-aie-aie!*

"I thought I'd have to worry about a *dog* when I came up here," he muttered nervously, moving away and wondering what life would be like with severed Achilles tendons.

"I chained the dog up in the barn when you said you were coming," I lied while trying to memorize his licence plate number.

But the geese had a docile side and Christine became quite fond of them, especially Beverley, who she invited into her garden to graze while she weeded. As long as she supervised them they were quite charming companions, content to hang around her and trim grass in return for the occasional choice weed, especially dandelions, which they demolished root and all with a loud, garbled honking. In the nursery portion of her garden she kept a garbage can full of water with willow twigs floating in it; willow (*Salix,* as in salicylic acid) is a natural aspirin, as good a tonic for little transplants as it is a cure-all for critters' aches and pains. The geese probably suffered from headaches due to excessive noise-making and always made a beeline for the willow water. Only occasionally did they get into trouble, when Christine turned her back or walked out of sight, but she always forgave them. Every time I told her I was fed up with them yelling at dawn or otherwise disrupting the peaceful farm routine, she would say: "Oh, but Beverley's so cute."

Geese love water, so it seemed cruel not to let them experience the pond in the back pasture. Christine opened the gate that secures the barnyard and herded them through. After a pleasant hour watching them splash about and perform passable imitations of swans, she became bored and tried to call them in. They ignored her. Late in the afternoon, with the other poultry gathered at the barn awaiting a handout, we tried again. Still no response. Unable to sleep that night, I looked through the back window and could see them sleeping peacefully on the water. The following morning they were honking at the gate, hungry. Wanting them at least to *play* a guard role, we refused to let them through the gate again. After a few days they'd forgotten about the pond and contentedly resumed their patrol.

We determined that Bev was the girl and Hilary the gander.

In mating season he became especially aggressive, hissing at me or chasing away the hens or the barn cat, and mounted Bev enthusiastically in pond or puddle. The pond, in this case, was the kind of cheap plastic wading pool popular in backyards of suburban homes (initially the geese had a pink one with submarines on it, but when it sprang a leak I took them to the store, where they picked out a blue one with a turtle motif, which we nevertheless still referred to as the Pink Pond).

Hilary's was a convincing performance, but it turned out that they were both girls. This became irrefutable when they built separate nests and laid eggs, sat them, and emerged disappointed a month later. We gave some money to the local evangelical church so the congregation would pray for them on Sundays ("Now let us pray for Hilary and Beverley, a homosexual couple seeking redemption"). We gave more to the local newspaper for an advertisement in the ANIMALS WANTED section:

TWO WHITE FEMALES SEEK MALE FOR
COMPANIONSHIP, POSSIBLY CHILDREN.

Summer turned to fall, but there was no response to the ad (beyond some heavy breathing on the phone). I was too busy to go to the auction to look for a likely suitor and then it was winter. It was not until March, with the scent of spring in the air and the wild geese fighting and mating in the back pasture, that Christine galvanized me into action and I finally began to have a gander for a gander.

One day, driving through the country in a direction I seldom travel, I noticed from a high point on the road a little hollow with a series of ponds and coops next to a ramshackle farmhouse. What appeared to be a large white bird was swimming in one pond. Doubling back, I discovered the New Goose Emporium and decided to purchase the only gander for sale — a bad move, perhaps, but the strange old goose rancher, dressed in the remnants of a Bible-black suit, assured me that the bird was hatched late and was too small to go to market for St. Thomas' Day (December 21) in accordance with the proverb "On St. Thomas the Divine, kill all turkeys, geese and swine." The young gander was a ragged-looking, mottled soul, obviously a crossbreed of the pure-white Embden with the squatter, grey-coloured Toulouse goose. Anyway, *my* goose was cooked, figuratively speaking, as it was February and soon Bev's sap would begin to run. I said I'd take him and I paid while the man's shawl-wrapped Scottish wife, cooing, "Oooooh, coom on Loosey Goosey, ye're goin' t' a fine neeuw home," stuffed the gander into a burlap sack.

Christine was initially appalled at the look of him, exclaiming, "This always happens when I send you shopping!" Eventually she softened and turned her attention to naming him, settling finally on Jethro, after the rock band Jethro Tull, I guess.

But in these modern times the Ugly Gosling doesn't turn into a swan and get the last laugh on his childhood tormentors. Instead he becomes a tormented misfit, blaming his violent tendencies on the circumstances of his upbringing and eventually receiving counselling. And was he aggressive? Indeed. He was my junkyard goose come to life; he even took on Arthur the rooster. However, he lost that fight and subsequently squeaked and ran away, his wings up if Arthur came too close. Having met his match, he began to settle down.

Geese mate for life, so before long Hilary, Bev and Jethro had formed an inseparable trio. Together they would toddle around the barnyard like sentries, Jethro and Hilary taking turns defending and attempting to breed Bev.

This state of relative calm persisted until a night in April when I was awakened by a *thump* and the yelling of the geese, who had been sleeping on the grass next to the house. I stumbled out into the black night, almost naked, waving the flashlight around and cursing. I could see through my half-opened, bleary eyes a couple of geese in the gloom. They were standing up and awake, but didn't appear panicked. Probably the owl had simply woken them. I scanned the blackness with the flashlight for a moment and, seeing and hearing nothing, went back into the house and crawled into bed again. Just two, I thought as I drifted back to sleep...and was that a *thump* I heard? If something had happened, there was nothing I could do until morning.

I woke up a little later than usual, realizing that the geese had not given their normal bugle call. I dressed and stumbled out into the grey light. I could see two geese near the barn, very subdued. Bev was in the goose version of a foetal position, white and still like a meringue, with her head curled over her back and tucked under a wing; only one blue eye was visible. Jethro roused himself enough to give a quiet honk, then sat down again. They didn't go and stand near the grain buckets as usual, sweeping the ground ahead of them with their long necks the way soldiers swing metal detectors to look for landmines.

Hilary was easy to spot in the short, early-spring grass: all that was left of her was a pile of feathers, a foot and a beak.

Before going back to the house to make coffee, I walked the boundaries and easily found the coyote's entry point on the side fence. The coyote had dug under, leaving all the loose dirt on the Millers' property. I walked around the Millers' pasture until I found the exit hole, and made a mental note to fill both of them with rocks. As it wasn't a foray in and out through the same spot, I hoped the raider was just passing through rather than returning to a den to feed pups.

"Thank goodness it was Hilary," Christine said rather uncharitably.

"They'll have a more normal relationship now," I suggested, hoping Bev and Jethro would be successful at parenthood.

I was sure Christine's unsentimental mood wouldn't last. Later that morning, after a visit to the barn and a few words with the bereft Bev and Jethro, she returned to the house and penned "Morte d'Hilary":

> Today we weep for Hilary
> Who didn't have artillery
> Nor yet a Don Quixote
> To challenge the coyote
> Who stole her in the night
> And put her friends to flight
> (Beverley and Jethro
> Who witnessed her in death throe)
> They now are sad as we
> Without goose number 3.
> Alas without a rescue
> She's just feathers in the fescue.

Bev and Jethro remained where they were for much of the day. But a day later everything was back to normal and they had turned the page, as it were. It wasn't callousness on their part, only lack of memory.

Jethro calmed down as he matured, although he was still raucous and wild compared with the pettable Bev, especially in the morning and when he received a handful of grain. No doubt he was merely protecting her. Usually I'd feed the chickens in the morning when I turned the sheep out into the fields. I'd also scatter a little grain around in the late afternoon when I let the sheep in and gave them their hay. But I couldn't convince the geese that there was a logical routine to it and was usually summoned whenever I made an appearance in the barnyard.

The house and the barn are about 50 yards apart. When I emerged and started walking to the barn they would follow, picking up speed and letting out bursts of high-pitched noise. After a few steps Jethro, who loved a parade, would get too excited and begin to run, with Bev thundering along behind, both of them squeaking faster and faster. After a few more steps they'd unfurl their powerful wings and, flapping furiously, roar by me about a yard off the ground. They flew rather like unguided missiles for which the concept of control, notably turning or stopping, is unknown. They almost flew, at full speed, right into the side of the barn. As they streaked by, I imagined them wearing leather aviators' helmets and goggles.

One day Christine and I were walking down the driveway toward the front gate, heading off for a walk in the park. Jethro and Bev had been grazing in front of the shack at the top of the driveway and spotted us when we were more than halfway to the gate, about 75 yards away. Jethro must have thought he was about to miss something, because he began to honk and run toward us, Bev in tow. Within a few paces they were airborne and closing the gap at a rapid rate. Bev managed to pull her wings back and slow enough that she landed at a half run, almost at our feet, but enthusiastic Jethro got his signals crossed. At the last second he pulled his wings back, but forgot to stop flapping and soared over our heads. I looked up to see a 20-pound farm goose passing overhead, staring down, his beak forming the word *oops*. He stopped flapping and, in a panic, partly retracted his wings, almost putting them across his eyes. His big body wobbled and began to drop and for a split second it looked as if he was going to fall out of the sky like an anvil. He got his wings partially spread again and crash-landed on the driveway almost at the gate, his landing gear buckled and his beak in the dirt.

He was no more competent as a stud. Like Hilary before him, but presumably with more appropriate equipment, he would climb into the Pink Pond with Bev, rub his neck elegantly against hers and clamber up onto her back to try to breed her. Bev was not at all good at this part, sometimes neglecting to lie down, which made it a rather steep climb. Eventually, though, Jethro would manage to scramble onto her back, grab her neck with his beak, drop his wings for balance and get himself into position. Their staccato shrieking would then change to a prolonged moan — a sound like a vacuum cleaner that's just ingested a plastic bag — interspersed with a few gasps for breath, climaxing with Jethro toppling sideways off her and landing with a big splash in the water. Certainly this year they'll have goslings, we'd say to each other.

When Bev began looking for a place to nest she had bad memories, I guess, of her previous, unsuccessful attempts with Hilary, and initially avoided the barn altogether. I put a pile of old hay into the Little Goose Coop, hoping to encourage her to nest there, but it was too far from the barn (and the food); she looked around inside the barn and dropped an egg into a pile of hay near the back, but never returned. She may have forgotten it, or discovered that the rats had rolled it away. She even rejected the purpose-built Fort Goose, an enclosure I had briefly locked them into after *la morte d'Hilary*.

Eventually she picked a spot in a sawdust pile that was directly in the afternoon sun. It couldn't have been much worse, as I had to rig up a burlap shade and every day or two spray her with water. It was all for nought. The eggs rotted and she eventually emerged, pale and unhappy, but greeted by an enthusiastic Jethro.

They had not managed to mate successfully in three years. I contemplated buying anatomically correct goose-education dolls at the farm-supply stores. There was also the XXX-rated video *Behind the Barn Door*, but the problem was perhaps not one that could be solved by anything less than surgery.

It was easier to do nothing. I think it's a mark of our maturity as farmers that we could accept them even though they were childless. What did we want more geese for, anyway? We spent so much time complaining about them. It's a variation on the joke about the friends who go to a resort: "The food's awful," says one. "Yes, and the portions are so small," says the other.

Roger the Ram

When the aged Yorkshire veterinarian and author James Herriot was trampled in his garden it was by ewes, rather than by bunnies or badgers or any of the other wild denizens of the English countryside. In another news item from that sheep-friendly island, a woman with a bale of hay on the back of her motorbike was forced off a cliff by rampaging, callous sheep.

Ewes can be strange creatures, very timid and standoffish until it's time for them to stake out a place at the feeder, at which time they'll bowl you over. I'm quite tall and thin, so carrying a bale of hay at chest height — which is just above the level a sheep can reach — makes me quite top-heavy and vulnerable to flattening and subsequent trampling. Many a time I've been putting hay into a feeder and have had ewes, which weigh as much as I do, but are compact and low to the ground, press me like a leaf between the pages of a scrapbook. One pushes in on the left, another on the right, then a third torpedoes right between my legs.

Rams have quite different personalities. Although he has the most potential to turn you permanently into a limper, your ram is usually the friendliest and most easily tamed of your flock. This is partly because, in most flocks, the ram is separated from the ewes until breeding season, a time he anticipates the entire year, but which occupies him for only a month in the fall. In the off-season, especially during the lazy days of summer, he gets used to your human presence and, even though you don't feed him anything other than the grass he's standing on, he becomes quite tame. Still, you shouldn't turn your back on him. By comparison, ewes are

most skittish in the summer and fall and only get slightly
tamer toward spring and lambing time.

Our neighbour's children, who were members of the local
4-H club, trained their young ram to a halter and walked him
up and down the road as if he were a 200-pound dog. Jan
disapproved of such behaviour; he had warned us not to try to
tame our ram and never to pet him. Rams, he said, are hard-
wired into certain behaviour patterns, such as charging and
butting rivals, and can become confused if they are patted on
the head, for example, at the same time as a young ewe is
sashaying by.

Christine found this "no-pat" policy extremely difficult to
accept, as she grew very fond of Eddie, eldest son of Eric and
Gladys and, in fact, the first lamb born on our farm.
Fortunately Eddie was a good stud, so I could maintain the
fiction that he wasn't really a pet even though Christine would
talk about him as if he were *our* firstborn. "Oh, he's such a nice
ram," she'd exclaim to our bewildered city friends as Eddie
lumbered up, three feet tall and 300 pounds, to get his nose
scratched. All sheep love a scratch and ours knew the location
of every rough tree and fence on the farm. Our neighbour,
who let his sheep mow his driveway, was amused at their habit
of polishing his pickup, until the day they removed the licence
plates. However, you don't often see a sheep scratching its nose
except with a hind hoof. A few of the ewes learned to push their
muzzles through the slats of their pen and wait for the geese
to come along and do the scratching for them. With their big,
saw-toothed beaks, the geese would chomp, honking loudly,
while the ewes stood stolidly, eyes rolled back into their heads,
occasionally twitching and kicking a back leg.

Eddie was a very gentle sheep, like his mother, and only once
or twice got aggressive during breeding season (when he picked
up a whiff of my faint, middle-aged testosterone.) He didn't

take a run at me, instead approaching at a half trot, dropping his head and lunging in a sort of feint. I put my hands out to catch the top of his head like a shortstop fielding a waist-high line drive, shouted "Bad!" or "No!" or something equally monosyllabic, then wagged my finger in his face and told him he'd be sausage if he didn't smarten up. Actually, compared with his dad, who had a very nasty streak, Eddie was about as mild-mannered as a ram could be. Neither ram ever threatened Christine, either because of her sex or her willingness to scratch their noses.

After a few years of breeding him, though, we simply had to make a change. We — the sheep, that is — were getting too inbred and I was concerned that there would be a marked decline in the flock's intelligence. We were noticing a slight increase in the number of weak, slow-growing lambs, a sign that you need some new blood. The problem was exacerbated by the fact that Eddie, depraved creature that he was, achieved the most multiple births when breeding his sister Eliza, his mother and his daughters.

It was midsummer, with still a couple of months to go before the ewes would need to be "serviced." Trying to be practical, I announced that Eddie was going to have to find a job on another farm with another flock. This would be a good career move for him, I claimed; he needed to broaden his CV and take on new challenges. My worst fears came true when it plunged Christine into a depression.

"I know, I know," she sighed, "we can't keep him, but we've got to find him a good home. He's not just going to go on the Ewe Haul truck like poor Eric." Eric had gone to a dark, air-conditioned room a few years earlier when his hoof problems became too difficult to manage.

"We'll do our best, but it's a buyer's market for rams," I cautioned.

"Maybe we can rent him out or lend him to someone and then get him back in a couple of years!" she suggested, brightening visibly.

"I'll try, honest."

Farm management and sentimentality are a tough fit. The job market for rams is quite bleak, there are few government retraining programs, and besides, I really didn't want to get attached to a ram, even a nice one like Eddie. After all, I couldn't say to him, "Okay, boy, I want you to think long term and go stand over in that field by yourself while we bring in Big Reggie to breed the ewes." His response would have been to take down the fence or the shepherd that stood between him and his rival.

Then we heard through the grapevine that Jan had sold his prize ram to a big ranch up north and, like us, was looking around for some new blood. As transparent as two pieces of Saran Wrap, Christine and I agreed to invite him over for a coffee one morning to see her garden — rose-growing was another of his interests. Somehow, I thought, I'd broach the subject of Eddie. Jan had had a good look at him when he was a lamb and had commented favourably on his straight top line (he wasn't swaybacked) and the quality of his fleece, but he hadn't been too impressed by the shape of his head. Jan was methodically trying to add characteristics to his flock of purebred Romneys that would improve their show quality. His biggest objection to Eddie was his pink nose; a classic Romney has a black nose, perhaps a minor point to a bystander.

Christine got Jan on the phone and was pleasantly surprised when he asked whether we still had that young ram he had once admired.

"I'll have a look at him then," he said in his matter-of-fact country manner and quickly said goodbye.

We were having coffee on the terrace in the sunshine. Finally, he mentioned casually that he had sold his ram and was looking for another one.

"Oh, really?" we both said.

"Eddie's got a good ROP," I said (you know, a good Record of Performance). "I've got all his breeding records."

"And he's such a swee...," Christine began until silenced by my glance. Jan wasn't interested in pets.

"No, no, that's okay — you got some good-looking lambs out there. The only problem is you didn't paper him when he was born." Register him as a purebred, that is.

"Maybe I should do that now."

"Can't. Too late."

"Oh."

"Doesn't matter to me though," he said, cracking a smile at the effect of his teasing. "I'm getting too old to care about papers or showing sheep. I'm just doing it for myself now."

We walked down to the barn where Eddie was whiling away the heat of the day, lying down, leaning heavily against the wall with his chin resting on a convenient concrete block. He raised his head slowly when he heard us approach, but made no attempt to get up or move away. It was only when I walked right up to him and grabbed him under the chin that he got to his feet.

I held him steady by cranking his chin into the air and burying his nose in my stomach while Jan checked his fleece, testicles hoofs and the meatiness of his back legs ("the paying end" of a sheep). We traded places while Jan looked at his teeth and felt around his jawline. Eddie gazed back at him blankly.

"I've been looking for the perfect ram for 30 years," said Jan, "and I haven't found him yet because he hasn't been born yet."

"What do you think of him?" I wasn't sure if Jan was implying

Eddie didn't make the grade.

"He won't put any meat on the back ends of my lambs, but I don't need that. I like his fine fleece though. He'll do."

He'll do. I knew Jan well enough to know that was the ultimate compliment.

We agreed on a price and a pick-up day and shook hands. Jan walked back to his truck, thanked Christine for the tour of the garden and for the coffee, opened the door and got in. "Pity about that nose though," he said, referring (I think) to Eddie, although I've received some comment over the years about *my* nose.

"I hope the black-nose gene in your ewes is dominant," I said. That was the limit of my scientific curiosity after hearing news reports about cloning and genetic modification.

We were delighted that the legendary Romney breeder in the valley, a man who had won all the blue ribbons for fleece, had bought *our* boy. And, amusingly, Eddie's sunny disposition even worked its magic on practical Jan.

"That ram of yours — what did you call him, Ed? — he's got such a nice personality," he told us a few months later. "He comes up to me when I'm working around the barn as if he wants to have a chat. He likes to have his nose scratched, too — did you notice that?"

Around the beginning of September I began to look for another ram. In the LONELY HEARTS section of the farm paper I placed an ad:

FLOCK OF EWES SEEKS RAM
FOR GOOD TIMES AND FAMILY LIFE.
MUST BE GENTLE.

However, none of the respondents had good numbers — a good ROP — and none of them was from a farm we knew. I didn't want to risk breeding a disease into my healthy flock. Jan agreed, which was probably why he gave Eddie a job; he could follow the lines back a dozen years through Killara, his own farm and the one that had sold us Gladys, without finding evidence of mad-sheep disease (known colloquially as "scrapie") or any other nasty surprises. People who routinely bought animals at the auction sometimes had to battle all sorts of afflictions in their purchases. Sheep suffer from many diseases, the first symptom of which is death, according to an old adage.

As fate had it, George and Pattie, a couple of old friends whom we hadn't seen for months, called and came out from the city for a visit. The conversation turned to friends of theirs, whom we knew only peripherally, and who were also raising sheep. Richard had inherited 100 acres of prime farmland and decided to make a radical career change. With his wife Maureen, he was raising two daughters on the proceeds of their family farm — no mean feat.

I recalled meeting them only a few times, at George and Pattie's Christmas parties, where they'd told me about the market for Easter lambs. Richard was in his 40s, a stocky man, ideally suited to sheepshearing. Maureen was lean with a long braid of greying reddish hair, looking as if she'd just stepped from the Irish countryside of her childhood. They had moved out to their property, which hadn't been farmed for a half century, and built a house while Richard maintained his city income. When their children were small and interested in the local 4-H club they filled their barnyard with chickens and a dozen sheep. Then, finding they loved the farm, they improved their flock and raised lambs for market. Richard sold lambs "by the each," custom-cut, to the customers he visited on his regular work rounds. At one point, he also had pigs and ducks for sale.

Sheep farming is a small world and the couple knew Jan quite well, having imported a couple of young Romney rams from New Zealand with his help. According to the story, Richard's ram had been so disoriented by the plane flight and reversal of the seasons that he had been unable to get up on his hind legs for the first year, leaving them with a flock of frustrated ewes. Jan's had been a good worker for several years until arthritis ruined his ability to earn his keep.

At one of the Christmas parties, Maureen had arrived alone. "It's Richard's shift in the barn," she'd explained with a tired smile. "We're lambing early to catch the Easter market."

"How many have you had so far?" I asked.

"Nearly 80."

Evidently sheep farming had ceased to be a hobby. Richard had even quit his job.

"Do you remember the New Zealand ram Richard bought?" Pattie asked now. I nodded.

"They haven't used him for years because they've changed their breeding program. They've still got him, though. He's become a pet."

"We've had some experience with people getting fond of rams," I remarked drily.

"We saw them a couple of weeks ago. Richard was asking how you were doing and wondered whether you could use him. The old ram, I mean."

"That sounds interesting."

"He's about 10 or 11 years old, apparently," said Pattie, "but Richard's sure he could still do his work." She chuckled. "He said he'd get a sperm test done if you were worried."

"I'd rather take his word on it. We need a ram around mid-October and I don't want to go to Rent-a-Ram."

"So Pattie told you about Aurora," Maureen said on the phone when I called.

"Aurora?"

"That's what we call him — you know, *aurora australis*, the southern version of the northern lights? It sounded like a New Zealand name."

"I *am* interested. We need new blood."

"You'd really notice the difference, I think, in your next set of lambs. They'd be a lot more vigorous — get up faster, grow better."

We agreed I would drop by a couple of days later and have a look at him. They weren't interested in money, but thought it would be nice for him to have some company and employment in his old age.

I arrived at their farm on an island in the river delta on a breezy day with just a trace of summer left in the low sun. The land was flat, protected on all sides by a dyke, with only a few tall trees and silos piercing the dome of azure sky. The leaves were tinged with yellow and russet, matching the colours of the pumpkins ripening in the fields and the summer's brown grass had thickened and begun to turn green. Rows of purple cabbage in an adjoining field added another colour to the autumn palette. White sheep dotted the pastures, like reflections of the puffy clouds.

The driveway crossed a deep drainage ditch, curved past some low coops for ducks and chickens, ran through a grove of trees and emerged near the house. A very large, modern barn with pale-green metal siding stood on one side of the driveway, while on the other a small pasture was divided by runs of electric fencing into small paddocks for the rams. Rows of ripened corn in the vegetable garden caught my eye. I got out of the truck and saw Richard, carrying a socket wrench in the crook of his arm and wiping his hands on a rag, walking toward me from an ailing tractor beside the barn.

I was very curious to see what a *real* sheep operation looked like, so Richard obliged me with a tour. He had 40 acres on one side of a small country road — the side including the house and barn — and 60 acres of fenced pasture on the other side. The main flock of 150 ewes, with 350 lambs born the previous spring, were on their own across the road. The remaining 50 ewes, all expected to lamb around Christmas, were in the field near the big barn, where they were easier to muster for inspections, extra feeding, and prenatal counselling. Pumpkins dotted another part of the field near the house, under a curious collection of scarecrows.

The interior of the barn was divided into two rooms, the largest of which was obviously winter quarters for the ewes. One corner of it was partitioned into a lambing area, with small pens set up along one wall much as we had. A large semicircle of hay feeders extended into the room and blocked the sheep's access to the bales of hay stacked 10 high along a wall. It looked very efficient, very professional.

"It's the only way the two of us can manage so many animals," Richard said ruefully. "We're pretty well maxed out here. The girls help, but they're busy with soccer and basketball and boyfriends. And school, I hope."

He took me through a doorway into the other part of the barn, which was stacked with more bales of hay and farm implements. In the middle, 12 feet tall and as enormous as an 18-wheeler, stood an old-fashioned combine harvester, a marvellous contraption of pipes and chutes and cutters and gears. With the addition of a propeller, it could have been a mad inventor's helicopter or an early flying machine.

"George mentioned you were growing your own grain," I said, somewhat awestruck. "So *this* is your combine."

"It's a long story," Richard laughed. "Grain is so expensive so I'd been wondering whether I could grow my own. I had just the right field for it. It needed to be ploughed and reseeded anyway because it wasn't producing good hay anymore. Then one day I was in the valley and there was a farm-auction sign — a foreclosure — and for once I wasn't in a hurry. Like stopping at a garage sale, right?"

He was smiling, but looking for confirmation, or perhaps sympathy.

"Go on," I prompted, dying to hear the punch line.

"Well, you know what auctions are like. I got there and they had all the equipment running in a big field. Tractors, generators, you name it, plus this thing. I stayed on a bit just to see what things were going for. Some of the equipment was in good condition, but I didn't *need* a new tractor. Then the combine came up on the block, and the auctioneer started the bidding at only $600. It got to $800 and I felt my hand going up. Then the bidding stopped."

"So you came home and said to Maureen, 'Guess what I bought, honey?' "

"Yeah, more or less," he chuckled. "But it ran all right and besides, I had the summer, which has its slow moments, to tinker with it. My neighbour seeded the field with oats. In the fall I combined it and fed the sheep for the year!"

I gazed at the combine and instinctively pulled my arms in tight to my body. I have an irrational fear of large farm equipment.

"I only did it for two years, though. It was too much of a hassle keeping it running and we found it was better just to buy a few tons of grain and get it delivered. Life is short. But it's worked out well for the school tours."

"The...?"

"School tours!" he laughed. "Last year, we were approached by a teacher with an elementary school class from Ladner, which *used to be* a farming town. You know how much teachers love a field trip. They gave us some money and we gave them a tour. I sheared a sheep and let them pet the lambs and run around in an empty pasture. They went away happy with a little more knowledge of where food comes from and why farms are important. And then the phone began to ring — other teachers, other schools.

"So now we're doing school tours several times a week. There's another one this afternoon. Maureen shows them the chickens and we always send the kids back with a few fertilized eggs for their science class. We've actually got to the point that we're running out of sheep to shear — last week I had to do half of a sheep in the morning and the other half in the afternoon!"

"Is that what the scarecrows are about?"

"That's right. Maureen sets up the pumpkin patch, the kids come late in the spring and plant their own and then come back to harvest it. Each class does a couple of scarecrows. Sometimes we have to replant — kids aren't used to disappointment these days."

"Great. Value-added farming!"

"City money, isn't it? More for an afternoon's field trip than we get for a lamb we raise for five months."

We walked out of the barn, crossed the driveway and made our way toward the rams. In one paddock was a blocky, white sheep that looked like a Romney. Richard, however, made for another paddock, in which a much more curious beast was roaming. Seeing us approach, he came up cautiously to within a foot or so of the electric fence.

"What is *this*?" I asked in a hushed voice. It was the weirdest-looking sheep I had ever seen: low to the ground, a feral face, like a cross between a pit bull and a ram. His clean, short coat of wool was more a pelt than a fleece. The beast's legs seemed to emerge directly from the corners of his rectangular back, so he bore a strange resemblance to a pool table. Sheep usually appear to have four legs underneath their centre, with the bulk of their wool making them look like a barrel. His huge scrotum, like a balloon filled with warm water, hung almost to the ground between his back legs. He stared intently back at us, with a look utterly unlike Eddie's benign, blank gaze, licked his lips and then turned around and lumbered back to where he had been grazing. His muscular thighs bumped together like a steroid-addicted wrestler.

"That's our best Texel ram," said Richard. "Isn't he a beauty?"

"Sure is," I said. "So that's what a Texel looks like." With that knowledge I could identify three smaller rams grazing in another paddock.

"What we do," he explained, "is use the Texel in the final crossbreed to put meat on the lambs. We couldn't make it with Romneys, because they're not prolific enough. The money's in meat now. The wool market has almost collapsed. Cotton is everywhere, even polyester's making a comeback and everybody's home and office is overheated compared with a generation ago, so wool clothing is less in demand. Bulk wool has gone from 50 cents a pound to 20 cents in the past year.

"The Romneys were our base flock, so we crossed them with Romanoffs to reinforce the multiple-birth gene." Richard gestured toward a group of rams in another paddock, presumably the Romanoffs. "We then took these crossbred ewes and bred them to the Texels to put the meat on them. As you know, the first generation of a hybrid is always the healthiest." I nodded. "It's worked well. We had 450 lambs from 200 ewes last year."

"How's your back?"

"Sore sometimes," he replied cheerily. "But look at the musculature on that Texel! You can pick a Texel carcass out of a whole line of lamb carcasses just by the meat on them."

We struggled to produce 25 lambs in a season and thought we were brave. This operation was almost 20 times our size.

"We'll go look at Aurora now," he said. "I'll just get a bucket and some oats."

We detoured via the barn to the Romney ram. Aurora's head shot up and at the sight of the tin bucket, he trotted over to the electric boundary.

"See how well he moves," said Richard. It was true. He had a very fluid gait, especially in the back end. A lot of sheep, including Eddie, tighten up a bit at the back end and lose their Marilyn Monroe walk when they're little more than lambs. Aurora looked very bright and alert for the sheep equivalent of an octogenarian. Richard swung one leg over the electric fence, then the other, and I followed suit. The ram trotted over, stuck his big head into the bucket and began to eat with a swishing sound like that of coffee beans stirred in a tin can. As he pushed his head down to get his lips onto the grain, Richard had to tug upward on the bucket to avoid being dragged to the ground.

"Only thing that's happened to him this year," he said, "is that all his teeth suddenly fell out." He chuckled; I gave an involuntary snort. "So you'd have to supplement feed with about half a pound of grain a day until the grass really gets going in the spring. He can't crop close enough to the ground now to get what he needs."

Richard put the bucket on the ground and, when the ram finished vacuuming the last of the oats and began to lift his head, he deftly put one hand under the chin and another on the rump to steady him. I prodded and pushed at a few of

Aurora's bits, as I'd seen Jan do with Eddie, and ran my hand along under his jaw, feeling for the lumps that signal a particularly virulent sheep disease called Caseous lymphadenitis, or CL. I pried open his lips and, sure enough, there wasn't a tooth in sight, but his mouth was a nice pink colour rather like a 1955 Cadillac's; he wasn't ravaged by parasitic worms. He was a gummer, all right, but all his equipment seemed intact.

"You know, I could get a sperm test done on him if you wanted," Richard said.

"No, no, that's okay. I'll just keep an eye on the ewes to make sure they're not coming back to him for more."

"Have you got a raddle?"

"No, I'll just put a blob of paint on his brisket."

Serious shepherds put on their rams a leather harness with a small holster at chest level into which they insert a coloured crayon, usually red, called a raddle. "Raddle" is a marvellous old shepherding word, like bellwether (a castrated ram who leads the flock), or beige (the colour of an unwashed fleece), that has come into regular usage. I had always understood the adjective "raddled" to refer to a woman who was tarted up rather imprecisely with rouge. A raddled ewe has red crayon smeared on her rump where the ram's chest, or brisket, lands when he mounts her.

Instead of buying a harness, I mixed some artist's pigment with a little mineral oil and daubed it onto the ram's brisket with a rag wrapped around the end of a stick. The effect was the same: you could see who had had a good time, mark a date on the calendar 147 days hence for lambing and, most importantly, see if she got another smear of paint in 17 days when, if she hadn't "settled," she would return. You could change the colour of the crayon just to be sure. If she kept coming back over and over again, either she had a health problem or the ram was firing blanks. A final point: rams are much more civilized than human males or roosters. They'll copulate only with consenting females.

Aurora looked fine to me, but I wanted a better name and was already debating: Randy? Roger? Roger sounded more English, the breed being originally from Romney Marsh in Kent. I asked Richard if Rog ... uh, Aurora, could stay where he was until mid-October; then I could take him home and introduce him to the flock.

⋗┈⊰⋗┈◯┈⊲⋗┈⋖

Richard's stock truck had been lent to a neighbouring farmer and, in any case, he was too busy with his cast of thousands (sheep and schoolchildren) to deliver Roger. But he did, he said, have a crate. I drove over in the old Toyota pickup on a cool October morning to claim my prize.

Roger was haltered and tied to a fence post in the driveway, looking like a very short pony. Richard had shorn his scrotum to cool it — making it less like a heated car seat — so his sperm would be as viable as possible. Maureen stood beside him, just close enough that his head brushed her leg, while Richard rounded the corner riding a big tractor. Nearby was a large box made of very sturdy plywood, a hammer and nails resting on top.

"We'll get him in the box, I'll nail it shut, then we can lift it with the tractor into your pickup," Richard announced. He positioned the unwitting beast in front of the box's opening.

"We better try to shove him in bum-first," he said. "You'll want to put a halter on him when you let him out because he's liable to come out like a freight train and hurt himself."

Like the linemen on a football team, we squared off against the ram and, on the count of three, began to push him backward into the box. Perhaps Roger thought he was going to be in one of those vaudeville shows where the magician saws the sheep in half or plunges swords into the box: for a moment, I thought he'd put a hoof against the far end. We finally over- powered him and got his woolly head inside. I held him while Richard grabbed the end panel and nailed it closed.

Richard slid the forks of the tractor beneath the box. The hydraulics easily lifted it and its 300-pound cargo into the air. After a little manoeuvring, he lowered it gingerly onto the back of the pickup, fitting it neatly between the wheel wells. I put the tailgate up.

"Take care of him," Maureen said in a sad voice. "He's been here for a long time."

"Oh, he'll have fun," I assured her.

Roger began kicking at the box, pawing at the sides and the floor.

"Better go," I said hastily. "I don't want him making a run for it on the freeway."

I drove as fast as I could, keeping one eye on the box in the rearview mirror. The box rocked and shook. People in passing cars looked at the truck with puzzled expressions. After an interminable drive (in reality less than an hour) I arrived home and soon had the truck backed up to the open gate of the ewe pen. They were, of course, out in the field, unaware of the surprise awaiting them.

With a pry bar I levered the nails out of the rocking box while keeping the end closed with my leg. If Roger had charged at that point, I would have ended up 10 feet from the truck. Opening the door just enough to get my hand and the halter in, I looped it behind one of his ears, then the other, working by feel, slid the front piece over his nose and pulled the loose end tight. He started forward, a bit hesitantly, then made a bid for freedom. The truck wobbled on its springs, but in a few seconds he had calmed down. I carefully backed toward the tailgate and, maintaining my pressure on the halter, clambered gingerly to the ground. He followed and I quickly pushed him into the ewes' pen, pulling the halter off his head and slamming the gate behind me as I exited.

For a few minutes he steamed around, exploring every corner and bellowing. I got a tin bucket with a couple of inches of oats and entered the pen, feeling like a trainee lion tamer. I rattled the bucket. No response. Roger continued to thunder around, confused by the strange surroundings. I rattled it again. He stopped. A third time. He trotted up to me and dived head-first into the bucket, nearly dislocating my shoulder.

At about five o'clock in the afternoon, as it was beginning to get dark, the unwitting ewes began to gather near the entrance to the pen. I had insisted they watch lambing videos on the Farm Channel before turning the TV to *All Creatures Great and Small*, but I was unsure whether they were prepared for a new ram. I corralled Roger behind some hurdles, reached over and daubed his brisket with a blob of paint, then flung open the gates. He brightened noticeably and let out a low moan.

There is great entertainment value in letting a ram loose with a group of ewes. Christine even came down from the house to watch Roger's excellent adventure. I pulled the hurdles aside and he rushed past me, his eyes as bright and hard as beads. Trotting enthusiastically from ewe to ewe, he savoured the perfume wafting from them like a wine taster ranking the latest vintages. The lambs we had kept for breeding took one look at his snuffling, grizzled head and wild eyes and ran for the opposite end of the pen.

Within perhaps half a minute he had checked out all 15 and pushed up against Mary's rear flank. She stood still and calm, with her legs braced, a serene expression on her muzzle. Roger heaved himself up onto her back, thrust himself into her, dismounted, sniffed at his work and hopped back up again. He was deliriously happy, his eyes almost glazed, his toothless old mouth open and his tongue hanging out.

For a few minutes Christine and I stood on the other side of the gate and watched, but we quickly tired of the spectacle and went back up to the house. Sex isn't a spectator sport. The following morning when I went back to the barn to let them out for the day, I counted three raddled ewes.

Richard and Maureen had been right — next spring's lambs were vigorous with the infusion of new blood. They included a boy from Mary that we thought looked like a keeper and named Jeff. You know, after the old comic strip *Mutton Jeff.*

A Poultry Gesture

When I first met Christine she was a vegetarian, one of the early 1970s varieties with bell-bottoms, long hair, tie-dyed shirts and a propensity for macramé and granola-making. She had come by her vegetarianism honestly, though, in that she had never liked meat — especially anything fatty, sinewy, or chewy. She had, for example, no need for veggie-patties that could be used to make *faux*burgers, as she never suffered from burger withdrawal. With just a little nudge from fashion — "living low on the food chain," and the book *Diet for a Small Planet* — she effortlessly made the transition away from meat. I wondered about her dietary preferences until she took me home to "the land of cake and steak" (Australia) and I saw that her mother's stove had only two settings: Off and Burnt. All became clear.

Living with her, I had become a sort of vegetarian-of-convenience, meaning that it was convenient to eat what she cooked. When it came right down to it, I was one of those people who would eat anything that cast a shadow and at restaurants and friends' houses I'd eat meat and enjoy it. Occasionally an acquaintance or neighbour like Marjorie or Beatrice, usually older women, would ask her sharply, "Well, you cook meat for *him, don't you?*" If she replied at all, she would say, "He's free to cook it himself if he wants to."

We weren't long on the farm before I realized that there were chickens that would need killing and either burying or eating — the odd misfit hen that discovered how good her own eggs tasted, the cockerels that had been hatched by broody hens and had no future in Arthur's one-cock town. Having grown up as the child of a child of the Depression, with Scottish blood,

I had learned to abhor waste the way Catholic children learn to fear the devil.

To minimize the stress on them and me, I decided to kill my chickens at night when they were asleep. Anybody who has ever spent time around chickens will tell you you're a fool if you try to catch them during the day, as their athleticism will exhaust you even as their panic demoralizes you. Much better to put on the pullet-proof vest, slip into their coop at night, lift one sleeping off its perch, stroke it a little while it *pok-pok-poks* quietly in your arms, still dreaming, and then awaken it suddenly with an axe. The plucking and the cleaning were not exactly favourite tasks, either, but once set up in the mudroom I could do about three in an hour. I tried to choose an interesting radio program to listen to during the task as I was in no position to change stations.

As a personal challenge, I set to work convincing Christine that chickens were vegetables. This is a fact known to many who have tried to have a conversation with both a chicken and a head of lettuce — neither gives a satisfactory response. As with our green vegetables, grown in our own manure-enriched soil, our chicken "vegetables" had grown up on good organic stuff, including bugs, worms, grains, greens and the leftovers from our fridge, including the carton of cream with "Best Before 1993" printed on it. As the chickens had spent happy lives, however brief, Christine discovered she had little resistance to eating them.

The grim pall of death that hangs over factory animals was not at all in evidence among our wandering flock. In my recollection of a visit to a broiler operation, where I looked out over a sea of panting white birds in a gloomy, darkened, windowless building that reeked of ammonia, the chickens had looked up at me with an expression that implored, "Take us! We're ready to move on to our next life!" What had a broiler

chicken done to earn such bad karma? Written how-to manuals
for VCRs? Designed the seats of our Honda Accord?

Not surprisingly, Christine limited herself to the white meat,
finding the dark meat too chewy and sinewy (a cockerel
is probably the equivalent of an Olympic athlete). However,
as there wasn't much breast meat on any of them we found
we were still going to the store. There, in the refrigerated
display case, watery, limp, tasteless breasts — pasty white with
the pallour of a life spent indoors without exercise —
beckoned us from the afterworld. Although we eventually
found a couple of farms that sold free-range, organic chickens, they were charging city prices and we were buying with
country money. Finally, after a considerable amount of
research, I found a source for broilers and began to raise
them myself.

Long ago, before the 1950s, most farmers kept a few hens
and a rooster to clean up the scraps, produce some eggs and
hatch some chicks, the pullets of which were kept and became
a new generation of hens, while the cockerels were grown out,
sometimes castrated as capons, for eating as "spring chicken."
Chicken was something of a delicacy, more expensive than
beef.

In the 1950s, chicken farmers became as specialized as the
wheat-growers on the prairies. Some raised throngs of laying
hens in batteries — in captivity — to maximize the egg production.
Others raised only broilers, a hybrid creature developed by
the agricultural companies, with the sponsorship of government
farm agencies and pharmaceutical companies. The broilers
were bred to put all their energy into meat, while the layers
were scrawny little things that nevertheless converted food into
eggs at a remarkable rate. By contrast our farm hens, the
old-fashioned "dual-purpose" Barred Rocks and Orpingtons,
produced a fair number of eggs and a decent meal, but

were hopelessly outdated by the production standards of the modern factory farmer. The boneless chicken breast, that standby of the modern restaurant industry, did not even exist when I was a child. Then, the classic chicken dinner was called "Chick'n Pick'ns," a scrawny, chewy bird cut up and deep-fried in batter.

The first year on the farm I raised about 50 broilers in a coop, inside a fenced-in run, on the opposite side of the barn from where the laying hens lived. Technically a breed called Cornish Giants, the broilers hatched as cute yellow fluffballs, but developed with astonishing speed. Within a few days they began to sprout white feathers at the ends of their downy wings. After a few weeks they were completely fledged but, unlike normal chickens, were ungainly and disproportionate. Winged pigs, as it were.

They grew fast, even on the organic regimen of cracked wheat, cooked barley from a local microbrewery and barrowloads of weeds and excess vegetables. By 12 weeks they looked like dinner (compared with about 25 weeks for a pure-bred cockerel), and spent their non-eating time gazing through the wire mesh at the hens of our permanent flock, who were wandering around "free-range" on the other side. Were they wondering about freedom themselves, or trying to figure out how they could get out and eat the hens? Although it was dirty and more difficult than anything else I'd done on the farm, raising them was a very Protestant experience, in that my three months of hard work was rewarded by a winter of excellent chicken eating and a number of happy friends who eagerly paid $15 a bird.

The following year, having had to turn down many a customer, I smartened up my operation, put a proper door on the coop, installed an automatic waterer, bought a half ton of milled grains from Ken, the local organic farmer, and started 100 chicks. With these numbers, I felt more like a real farmer than an idle hobbyist. At night they packed themselves into the coop for shelter and, as they grew, occupied every available inch of the floor. I had to move *very* slowly around the coop, making sure they weren't disturbed, for I had heard about "piling" — panicked chickens (or turkeys) running into the same corner, trampling (and then eating) the "early birds." Even low-flying planes can precipitate piling, although as the broilers were outside during the day and had a tree to hide under, that wasn't one of our problems.

The smell was absolutely appalling and I soon realized I was having trouble putting enough food into the feeders to satisfy them. My mix of fibrous grains, especially the barley from the brewery, afforded them only temporary satisfaction; they would often wait for me like a school of piranha. If I was ever more than an hour late with breakfast, lunch, dinner, or between-meal snacks, they'd descend upon me, biting and pecking at the bucket, my legs and my feet and when I poured the grain into the feeder they piled up onto it like football players chasing a fumble on the one-yard line. Then I went away for a couple of days, neglecting to tell Christine to change from her shorts into heavy jeans and gumboots when she went to feed them. She was furious with me.

"Never again," she swore, "will you raise this many and leave me in charge. I was almost dragged down."

I imagined the headline in the local paper:

FARMWIFE EATEN BY POULTRY
90 Broilers in Custody

The first year, when it had come time to slaughter the broilers — a process usually referred to as "processing" — I brought my entire educational background to bear on the matter of the plucking and the cleaning and realized, by dividing three birds per hour into 50 birds, that the flies and I were going to have a very long day. Subsequent investigation led to a legendary local character named Al, a chicken processor who made house calls in his full-size, fully equipped Ford pickup (with Abattoir options, available from your local dealer). After an astonishingly violent hour I was left $70 poorer, but with all my chickens plucked and cleaned and cooling in water barrels. All I needed to do was bag them and freeze them.

Then in his late 20s, Al was a clean-shaven, neatly barbered, well-spoken young man who had been a professional chicken slaughterer since he was 14 and had had to be driven to work after school by his mum. His was not an example of options I'd seen at school on Career Day ... car salesman (plaid jacket), chartered accountant (suit jacket), but no chicken slaughterer (rubber apron). I was to discover that he was at least as well known around the valley as the mayor.

"Al do your chickens?" people would ask when they discovered we were raising broilers. "Great guy — nobody does their own anymore. It's not worth it."

He also did turkeys, ducks and geese. It was so much better to get him to pay a visit than to take a huge cage of them to one of the processing plants, where a chicken goes in one end of the assembly line and comes out the other anonymously; as mine were fed and exercised with such care, I wanted to make sure I got to eat them.

The second year, with about 90 birds left out of the 100 I'd started with, I invited Al and his assistant over. Once again I marvelled at their efficiency: chop, stuff into a vertical metal cone for draining, toss into a vat of hot water to loosen the feathers, hold the ex-bird by the feet against a revolving drum covered in rubber fingers to pluck it, gut it, cool it. Throughout it all they carried on an animated conversation about movies, local politics, travel and the weather, pausing occasionally to hose the blood and feathers off their butchers' aprons. It took them about an hour and a half to get everything done and packed away, then they were off to their next farm.

So there I was, around noon on a stinking hot August day, sitting in the shade beside the barn with an array of clean garbage cans and buckets around me. As the key to freezing a chicken is to cool it gradually (so the meat "stands away from the bone," as old farmwives say), I spent a few hours changing the water while I pondered this rather bizarre business. Both Christine and I had become dependent philosophically on a freezer full of our own food, on roasting a chicken for a winter dinner and serving it with parsnips dug from the frosty garden. In the candles' glow, with a crackling fire in the woodstove, even the rats seemed far away.

But getting Al over was a problem, as all the chickens had to be ready at the same time: some were a couple of weeks behind the others, and were less than keen when I called for volunteers. And then there were our customers, some of whom had enthusiastically ordered a half dozen and claimed to understand that they *had* to be picked up on the processing day.

"Can you keep mine until the weekend?" one asked. "I've got a golf game and then appointments for the rest of the week."

Another said she couldn't possibly make it out to the farm because she was at home waiting for Molly Maid to show, so could I possibly bring them by? I ended up parking two dozen chickens in a neighbour's freezer and resolved in future to do just enough chickens for ourselves. After all, it was a poultry gesture to the city's food supply.

In a further refinement, I decided to grow far more corn than we could possibly eat and time it so that the broilers would eat little else for their last week or two. Corn matures here at about the beginning of September, so I bought a couple of dozen broiler chicks as day-olds in the middle of June, from the local hatchery. Twenty broilers is about as many as we'd eat in a year: when your chickens average six pounds, you end up eating almost as many leftovers as you do in the week after Christmas.

Al had remarked during one of his visits that he was at home one day a week, a convenient option if I had just a few to do and wanted to avoid paying his travel time. About a week after I started feeding corn, I figured it was time to give him a call.

"Ah, yes," he said, remembering me. "It's about time for our annual visit."

"You still having your day at home?"

"Yeah, Tuesdays. How many you got?"

"Ten."

"Is 9:15 okay?" I grunted affirmatively and he gave me an address. "Just come down the side driveway. We're around the back."

On Monday evening, I set up my portable cage on the back of the old pickup. The cage was made of light wooden frames with wire mesh stapled to them and tied together with baler twine. It had no bottom and was useful also as a quarantine station. With the addition of a heat lamp it had been the first home for these broiler chicks; they started and ended their lives in the same cage. I put a water bucket inside and scattered straw on the floor as a mattress. Two cleaned garbage cans occupied the space between the cage and the cab.

With the death truck ready, I went back to the house and waited for it to get dark. Then, moving as quietly as I could, I went into the coop with the flashlight and picked out the ones I wanted, carried them quietly past the sleeping sheep and put them into the cage. For a moment they shoved each other and squabbled, but they were soon asleep again. In 10 minutes I was back inside.

After breakfast the following morning, I filled the water barrels, started the truck and set off down the country roads to Al's place. I drove slowly, as the chickens seemed to be enjoying the view and I didn't want them wind-burned. A commuter in a BMW tailgated me on the winding road until some bits of straw and feather stuck to his windshield.

Al's place was easy to see even before I could read the address, as his roadside metal mailbox had been modified with brightly painted wooden wings, tail feathers, and a beaked head with red wattles and a comb. The house itself was a modest bungalow quite near the road, with one short driveway that went almost to the front door and another driveway just past it. Behind the house there was a cleared half acre bordered by woods. It contained a large, fenced vegetable garden and, on some rough lawn in the shade of a tree, Al's big Abattoirmobile. In one corner, in the shade of a small grove of trees, was a shed. A couple of men in rubber aprons and boots were joined by others standing nearby with their hands in their pockets.

In my rearview mirror I could see Al's assistant put down the chicken he was gutting and guide me with hand signals as I backed slowly between the trees. At his bidding, I stopped the truck and got out.

"Hi! Great day, eh?" Al declared enthusiastically, referring presumably to the warm September sunshine. The other customers, middle-aged and rumpled in their farm clothes, nodded acknowledgement.

"I'll just be a minute," Al said. "You're next." He had better time-management skills than my doctor, though there was no waiting area with a pile of 1953 *Reader's Digests*.

When it was my turn, Al took my dozen and worked swiftly. Fifteen minutes later I noticed another pickup in the driveway — the 9:30 appointment.

"Are you busy like this all year?" I asked Al.

"We got our steady clients," he said, "but we always shut down for January and February. Everybody knows that. People like you, who are just doin' it for themselves — reducing their cost of living — that's mainly a summer and fall thing."

"You go away in the winter, then?" I asked.

"Oh, yeah," he said, smiling, his eyes softening. "I always travel. Last winter my girlfriend and I spent six weeks in Costa Rica. I spent a winter hitchhiking through Asia, I've been all over South America...."

"Have you ever been to Australia?" I asked, thinking about Christine and our trips together before we tied ourselves down with all the livestock.

"Yeah, I was there a few years ago and really enjoyed it. I'd like to go back, but there's still a lot of the world I want to see."

Al walked over to guide the next truck backing into position beside me. A dozen or so big geese honked excitedly in the cage on the back, pleased to have gone for a drive in the country.

"Where are you going this year?" I asked him.

"Well, my girlfriend and I might just get a place in Fiji for a month or so."

"Have a good one," I said, getting into my truck. "I've got 10 more to do in two weeks, then that's it for me this year."

"Okay, you call me this evening — I don't have my appointment book here."

I was back home less than an hour after I'd left.

Still Life

Although she enjoyed sharing the place with the sheep and the chickens and looked after them very capably whenever I went away, Christine left them to me to manage. But she was always willing to help if I needed an extra pair of hands to, say, hold down a ewe that had a stuck lamb or clip the wings of a rogue pullet. As part of the package of farm life she even endured the most harrowing chores, such as holding day-old lambs and comforting them while I docked their tails with a device called a Burdizzo (which doubled as a castrator and could easily have belonged to a museum of medieval torture instruments).

For better or for worse, in farming as in marriage. If I was able to make myself do these things, she would help when I needed her, and I loved her for it. She knew I was really a softie who loathed the causing of pain, the culling and the killing, tasks I was only able to accomplish because I'd watched lots of TV and played video games.

It didn't help that most of the animal disasters happened when I was away, usually travelling and painting for a commission or project. Working, yes, but also enjoying myself.

"Don't worry, Pioneer Woman's got everything under control," she'd say tersely over the phone. "Pioneer Woman" was code, encrypted like a credit card number sent over the Internet.

"Oh, no, what's gone wrong this time?"

Once it was a lamb that had missed drenching — that is, I had somehow overlooked it when I was worming all the others — and collapsed in the pasture. Another time it was Eric knocking down the fence and impregnating the neighbour's spinster lawn mower. Or Bruce the duck losing his head. Fortunately she was resourceful and the neighbours were helpful and tolerant.

After all, the animals were *my* hobby; Christine had wanted to move to the country primarily to create a garden. It was her growing passion for gardening that, in large part, prompted her to lose interest in and eventually quit her city job. She was much more interested in the acre of pasture on the south side of the house and its potential to become a grand garden than she was in either the condition of the house itself or the property's potential for raising critters.

Wherever we were, she had always tried to plant a few bulbs or shrubs around our home; once, she dug a small plot in the backyard, planted it with tender lettuces and basil and then watched as busloads of slugs and snails arrived to mow them flat. My role in this nascent activity was to supervise, meaning I'd watch her and occasionally offer compliments like, "That's nice, dear." I was normally underneath a car or a sink and remained steadfastly uninterested in gardening until, soon after I crossed the magic threshold into my 30s, we moved to the Kerrisdale house and inherited its cottage garden. With Christine taking the lead, we set out to maintain the shrubs and flowers. I did my part using the let's-see-if-this'll-work method, while she read, took courses and sought advice from the handful of our friends who knew which end of the trowel to hold. Within a year, we were hooked.

There are gardeners and there are *gardeners*. I was one of the former. I had absorbed the fundamental lesson of planting — "green side up" — and enjoyed fussing around with a few plants, especially irises and poppies that were pure colour suspended in the wind. But Christine studied the subject from the ground up and found that even her classical education, including the Latin she had learned in school and the literature she had read, could be incorporated into her study and appreciation of botany and garden design.

The first visit to Monet's Giverny not only inspired her to attempt a pond garden, it influenced the style of cottage garden she wanted to develop on the farm. She wanted the formality of Monet's main garden incorporated into the design of her own. As we already had the axial framework of a country property stamped onto our land, including fences and cross-fences and the driveway lined with poplars, we made a long, formal *allée* the central feature of her garden. As at Giverny, it ran for 100 yards from in front of the house to the fence near the road.

Giverny was Monet's abiding passion for the last 35 years of his life, and Christine came away convinced that she, too, must somehow devote herself to such a task. Her only concern was that she had left starting this, her life's work, until it was too late. A supportive spouse, I assured her that she had lots of time, pointing out that Colonel Sanders didn't come up with his batter recipe until he was nearly 65.

Old-fashioned, antique roses were favourites and provided the structure for the new garden. Of all the plants one could stick in a garden, old roses meant the most to her. Not only were they relatively easy to grow and maintain, they also were replete with literary and cultural associations that went far beyond aesthetics. There was *Rosa eglanteria*, the eglantine of Shakespeare's time with scented leaves; Ispahan, an ancient Persian variety used for making attar of roses; Mutabilis, a China rose; *Rosa sancta*, the Holy rose of Ethiopia; Autumn Damask, alleged to be the rose mentioned in Virgil's *Georgics* as flowering twice a year near Paestum, the ancient Greek colony south of Naples. Most had relatively small flowers and a subtlety of perfume and colour that made them excellent garden plants; they fitted in well on the gentle slope in front of our low-slung abode, among the classic cottage perennials that included irises, poppies, peonies, foxgloves and hollyhocks.

Many of these roses were bred or collected in France in the 19th century, some by Napoleon's Empress Josephine, and had mellifluous, romantic names such as Adelaide d'Orléans and Duchesse de Montebello. Fantin Latour, a sturdy bush covered with ruffled pink blooms, got its name from the Barbizon-era painter. Gloire de Dijon, a creamy yellow climbing rose, was the subject and title of a D.H. Lawrence poem. Its first stanza reads:

When she rises in the morning
I linger to watch her;
She spreads the bath-cloth underneath the window
And the sunbeams catch her
Glistening white on the shoulders,
While down her sides the mellow
Golden shadow glows as
She stoops to the sponge, and her swung breasts
Sway like full-blown yellow
Gloire de Dijon roses.

During the winter, when there was little to do beyond dreaming of next year, there were garden books, including the writings of Gertrude Jekyll and Vita Sackville-West and modern gurus such as Peter Beales and Penelope Hobhouse. Gardening became more than Christine's hobby, more even than her vocation. It was her passion.

She continued to volunteer one day a week at a botanical garden in the city, taking with her our extra eggs and vegetables to sell. I passed the time with my painting and the regular work with the critters. Once a week or so, especially during the winter, I'd go into the city too, do a little shopping at the specialty stores, buy myself lunch, drop by the gallery to see if they'd sold anything, then beat a retreat home before rush hour.

Having joined the local rose society, Christine was able to obtain some rare examples by growing cuttings taken from the members' long-established gardens. She imported others from England. When we travelled out into the country along back roads and past abandoned homesteads, she was always prepared for rose-rustling. With her secateurs, some empty jars, and some water, she took clippings from roses established 50 or 100 years earlier, then grew them out in her nursery and planted them in the garden.

The first few years were backbreaking. I had bought a good rototiller from a woman whose attempts at country living had evidently led to a divorce and her return to the city, and we set out to break up the turf compacted by years of pacing and grazing by cattle and horses. Like a prairie sodbuster behind his plow, I walked behind the tiller, leaning with all my meagre weight on its handlebars to try to keep the revolving tines in the earth. Inevitably they hit a rock or bound in the sod, causing the rototiller to take off like a drag racer with me pulled along, legs almost horizontal behind me. But we kept at it, labouring together on the days when I wasn't slaving elsewhere on the fences, the pens or the pastures.

Finally, after a few years during which the garden was little more than skimpy plants growing on a big field, it began to fill in. You could no longer see from one side of it to the other and the pattern of "rooms" and pathways emerged within the tall borders and rose hedges. To add structure to it, we erected a large pergola, 10 feet wide and eight feet high, along the upper third of the *allée* to provide support for more than a dozen climbing roses, an arbour and some paving. Taking a leaf from Sackville-West's Sissinghurst, we laid out the adjoining beds quite formally; Christine planted them in a riotous, almost random blizzard of cottage colour. For contrast she planted one square bed entirely with lavender, set within a "room" with walls made of a hedge of tall roses. Another rose hedge provided a transition from the formal beds to the rougher pasture grass; higher than my head, it became a mass of bloom every June and July, pink, purple, and white, perfumed and alive with honeybees drunk on nectar and bumbling in the sunshine. It was glorious with the summer breeze sighing in the poplars and the birds feeding and singing among the flowers.

As the heavy work in her garden diminished, we agreed that I would take over the vegetable garden, leaving her with unfettered time for the roses and the nursery she was developing apace. It made sense, as I was becoming more and more like a vegetable. At least, I did enjoy lining up the vegetables in rows like soldiers.

We were the only people on the road who had any sort of flower garden and apparently were perceived by some to be wasting good horse pasture. One day when Christine was working in the shrubbery near the road she heard the *kaklop, kaklop* of horses walking slowly and the faint murmur of conversation from the two riders. As they came a little closer she could hear their voices more clearly.

"Looks like a nice place," one was saying, "but if it was mine I'd get rid of all those shrubs."

"Over my dead body," Christine declared, rising from among the flowers.

When it came right down to it, we were also almost the only people on the road who had a real farm, with a mix of animals, a regular cycle of births and deaths and a traditional view of how the country operated before supermarkets and long-distance commuting came along. Most of our neighbours just had horses and a complement of dogs and cats. Never was this more evident than the day Christine, working near the foot of the driveway with the assistance of the poultry, looked up to see a horse and rider standing stock-still on the road just outside the gate. The horse was staring up the driveway, fixated, as animals do when something unexpected enters their world.

"Can I help you?" Christine asked, wondering if the horse had ever seen a gardener before.

"It's okay," the rider replied. "It's just my horse has never seen a chicken before." When the horse had satisfied itself on the matter of the chicken, it allowed the rider to resume control.

The response to the garden varied widely.

"What do you *do*, Christine?" she'd be asked by acquaintances. From the perspective of many busy city people, there's not much happening in the country to occupy the time between meals.

"I've got a large cottage garden, mainly old-fashioned roses — the type that have a beautiful perfume. I sell rosebushes, give garden lectures ... that kind of thing."

Usually the response was rhapsodic. Few people past the age of 30 with three-digit IQs ask whether she misses tearing off to the office every day.

However, when visited by strangers, including many gardeners, she often gets a different response: "What a lot of work!"

To which she always replies, "No, what a lot of pleasure!"

When garden clubs began to call and ask if they could tour, and a national television program did a feature on the place, it became evident even to the skeptical Christine that she had created something out of the ordinary. As with English country estates of yesteryear, the pleasure garden stood in the midst of a working farm, with the manure from the animals and the clippings producing a rich compost to be ploughed back into the soil year after year. In a world becoming obsessed with concepts of sustainability, we were so old-fashioned as to be state-of-the-art.

>–!–◆>–O–<◆–!–<

Although the animals fed us and entertained us, and we made a little cash selling eggs, lamb and vegetables to our city acquaintances, we couldn't make a living from the farm. In an age when even skilled family farmers were going bankrupt, I knew enough not to burn the bridges to my urban *métier*. This meant continuing to paint and exhibit in the city.

Besides, we knew that if we farmed intensively we'd be contributing to the destruction of the countryside, the balance between nature and agriculture, that had drawn us away from the city in the first place. Although by the government's agricultural standards we were a Mickey Mouse operation, a true hobby farm, we were nevertheless producing nearly the maximum amount of pollution for a property of our size, in the form of nitrates from the animals' manure.

Before we moved to the farm, I had spent most of my time painting city scenes and other landscapes for the gallery and books. However, I did pass some time painting the garden and the house where we lived, and liked painting watercolours when we travelled, sometimes daubing little *pôchades* into sketchbooks, other times painting more formally, framing the results and hanging them at home. If the memory they represented faded I sold them and I ended up keeping just a few from each place — the front porch of the Kerrisdale house, the doorway of a cottage we'd rented in the Languedoc, our Renault parked under a tree on a blazing summer day, a string of rowboats in the harbour at Santa Margherita Ligure, Christine sunbathing on a sandbar along a secluded creek — personal memorabilia, infused with the glow of time spent together. Paintings that were going to have meaning for me in my dotage had to be from *our* world, indeterminate enough that the memories of our youth could fill in the blanks. Watercolour was the perfect medium: shadows defining unfinished forms, loose brush-work, paper left unpainted, soft washes.

I recognized Monet's influence in the way Christine began planting her garden and grooming the pond, and felt the same influence affecting my perception of the farm and the animals. No, I didn't grow my beard to my navel and cart large canvases across fields to paint haystacks in the blazing sun. But I'd absorbed the fundamental lesson of Giverny: Monet had created a paradise that then became his muse.

Nowhere was this more evident than at his famous pond. He had started with a blank canvas and created a *character*. Adding another level to his examination of whether life imitates art, he erected a Japanese-style arched bridge and included it in a number of his canvases. Near the end of his long life he painted four huge, almost abstract canvases of the pond's surface for the circular gallery at L'Orangerie in Paris. His art had become inseparable from his life in the country.

In a modest parallel with *vieux* Claude, I started painting the farm, focusing early on the animals and their curious habits. Like Edward Hopper's wife, Christine wouldn't let me hire a nubile young model, so I was forced to orient myself toward the birds and the beasts if I wanted to paint anything more animated than a cabbage. The subjects lacked the overlay of rootlessness and ceaseless, purposeless change that had influenced me in the city. Since art school, where I'd failed Angst 101, I'd tried to keep my sunny disposition to myself.

One winter day, ploughing through an Australian magazine her sister had sent her, Christine came upon an article about an artist named Greg Hansell who lived with his wife and some chickens in the parrot-flecked shade of some gum trees near one of the colonial-era towns not far from Sydney. The photographs showed a burly, bearded guy standing in a dusty farmyard with a few hens pecking around his feet. In the background was a tin-roofed shed that served as his studio. His media were linocuts, watercolour and pastels, the last done with crayons he made himself using natural materials found on his own land and on his travels. Owning hens, he should have painted in egg tempera. As should I.

"Looks like me," I said when she showed me the article.

"I am not afraid to do pretty things anymore ... ," Hansell stated. "I don't tend to think about the psychology side of it. Some artists do seem to be meaningful in a lot of ways. But the whole reason for doing a painting is that you wander around and you think, 'Gee, that looks nice,' so you sit down and paint it. It's fairly elementary."

"Sounds like me, too," I said.

I found myself observing the animals as I worked around the barnyard, getting to know their habits and their poses so well that their images became fixed in my mind. Chickens with their heads down and tail feathers in the air, forming a shape like a candle flame. Their hunt-and-peck motion (not a keyboard technique). The sheep, stoned by chewing their cud — an action that releases endorphins — contented like cows in old milk advertisements, casting long blue shadows, grazing quietly as the sun set and washed the world with its golden brush. A hen standing in the harsh winter sun, looking three-dimensional and real but casting a distorted shadow like a cartoon silhouette.

I found it best to draw them quickly, like a Zen sage with brush and ink, when I could find a perch above their normal line of vision, or look for them in snapshots of the farmyard, then paint them more formally in the studio when I had time on my hands during the winter. The chickens, living as they did in a world of their own, were the easiest to record, while the sheep, being the essential prey species, were wary of anybody coming onto their turf. The geese were hopeless; they were incapable of ignoring me and going about their business, so I was reduced to using snapshots taken surreptitiously.

In art as in physics, the Heisenberg uncertainty principle rules. It says, more or less, that you can't measure something without changing what you're measuring; in art, you can't sit down and paint a critter without the critter noticing you and coming to see if you've got some food to share. However, if I sat among the hay bales in the barn I could observe without being observed. In the fall and the winter, when we let the sheep graze the grass around the house, they were unaware of me working on the other side of the window as they munched, snoozed, socialized, and fertilized.

Spring was a hopeless time for painting, as we were busy with planting and lambing and repairing winter's depredation. In summer I sketched, hanging about the farm with brush and ink or watercolour, or ranged around the countryside painting scenes for the gallery. Returning to the city for the day, I painted along the harbour and the beaches or sketched humans going about their business. In summer and fall I also travelled, sometimes accompanied by the patient Christine, painting commissions or working on book projects but always filling a watercolour sketchbook with ideas for later. Then, in winter, with the woodstove stoked and the lamps lit, I got to work.

It was the combination of art and experience on the farm that seemed so refreshing after the city. When we were urban, I'd concentrate for a while, then put down the tools and wonder what to do. Stroll in the garden for two minutes (it was a small garden)? Walk the couple of blocks up to the shops? Grab a coffee? Read the paper? Meet friends? Get further distracted by looking for something to buy? Eventually I would return home and try to pick up the threads of what I was doing.

On the farm, the work outside and the art inside seemed to merge seamlessly: throw the leftover scraps to the chickens, put some hay in the feeders for the sheep, go back to work. Stretch the legs by walking the boundaries. The days drifted by, with the time spent farming a perfect foil to the time spent painting. In fact, with farming occupying the body so completely, the mind had more time to develop ideas. That is a lesson from Chinese Zen art, recorded in the *Mustard Seed Garden Manual of Painting*: think first, then paint. The act of painting is an anticlimax.

Unlike Monet, it took me a long time to begin painting the garden. Six or seven years after we moved to the farm, when the garden was really filling in and developing the sort of structure that makes for good composition, I began to sit in it and daub some watercolour onto a sketchbook. But I was afraid to be too focused. As I sat in its cheerful, dappled light, I found myself wondering whether this was a first step toward weaning myself from the farm and the garden, much as I had done with previous places where we had lived. If your home is up on the wall, along with the other places you've lived and travelled, is it time to move on and start over? As long as I didn't finish the *pôchades* in my sketchbook, or keep any of the finished watercolours, we would be unable to leave.

For much of the year, when I emerged from my studio or the barn and wanted to play "find your wife", I looked first around the garden, where I would eventually find Christine clipping and pruning or digging and rearranging, or tending the cuttings she was growing out for her nursery and selling to her visitors and fans. In the winter I would find her pinned to an old wicker chair next to the woodstove, her lap shared by a cat and a weighty garden tome. It was enough for us to lead together such a simple life.

The Grass Is Always Egregious

The experience of visiting Richard and Maureen's farm had been a bit unsettling. They were *really* farming, completely engaged in the effort to improve their stock and market it. In short, they were serious, while I came away feeling I was a dilettante, an amateur, an appropriate word that has its roots in the Latin verb *amare*, "to love." For, irrespective of how successful we were, we loved being on the farm, soaking up the animals' wisdom and feeling more connected with the real world than we ever had when living in the city.

Our former life now seemed artificial. There, food was delivered by truck from a warehouse to my local store and was always there when I zipped in to look for something at the last minute. "Country Style" meant something unfinished or rustic but blisteringly expensive in a furniture "shoppe," and a "country-style breakfast" meant BIG. What season was it? Were the neighbourhood children in school? Did the newspaper ads describe Fall Fashions, which meant it was early summer, or the Spring Collection, which meant it was the dead of winter? Were the Christmas decorations going up in the stores? Then it had to be October. Did people have suntans? Must be January.

When it came right down to it, I still loved the city and enjoyed the parade of people and the frenetic pace at which they lived their lives, as long as I wasn't sharing a roadway with them during rush hour. I was urban to the core and knew it; I realized that the old saying, "You can take the boy out of the country but you can't take the country out of the boy" had its urban counterpart.

Nevertheless, we continued to enjoy the farm in spite of occasional restlessness. In the summer I got fed up with cutting the lawn around the house and garden, and with mowing the fields to restart the pasture grasses for the fall. Winter was worse: the weather was fairly lousy by mid-November and it would be early in March before it could be counted on to brighten and stir with the promise of spring. On cold, rainy days I'd find Christine staring out of the window, dreaming of wearing shorts and a T-shirt on an Australian beach or in a garden. But with the return of spring, the birth of the lambs and the reinvigoration of the chickens, we eagerly replanted the vegetable garden and started again. When there were still root vegetables rather than rot vegetables left in the ground or the cellar, we congratulated ourselves on having grown enough food to get us through the winter. Once farm life meant eating salted mutton and turnips for the two months before the spring crops grew, feeling your gums get all punky with rickets. We did cheat by buying some California-grown greens during the winter though.

But was this *it*? Had we really settled down, or was this just another phase? Would we stay on the farm until hauled off to the old-folks' home to dream away our final years?

><del>+</del>+<del></del>+<del>O</del>+<del></del>+<del>+</del>+<

We had other friends besides Richard and Maureen who'd cashed in their city chips and taken up farming. Perhaps, we thought, it was time to pay those friends a visit to find out how they were doing. Were they happy because they were engaged in full-time farming? Were we just too easily bored and restless, exemplars of the been-there-done-that gener-ation? We hadn't so much lost touch with them as found ourselves, and them, just too busy to visit. If our farm exhausted us, we could scarcely imagine what *theirs* was like.

In fact it was easy for us to get away for a couple of days, as long as we did it between the beginning of June, once we had determined that all the lambs were healthy, and November, when we started bringing the sheep in at night. I suppose we could have called the local pet kennel — "What would you like to board with us, sir? Fifteen sheep and 30 chickens? Very well, that will be $300 a night." — but there was no need for that Plan B. The sheep would graze in the sunshine and snooze under the stars, while the chickens would be safe and relatively content in their coop with its attached outdoor run. It was easy to put out a couple of days' worth of grain, admonish them not to eat it all at once, and then lock them in rather than allowing them to wander around the farmyard. A phone call to Chuck and Angela, asking them to have a look our way a couple of times a day for circling crows or buzzards, completed the preparations.

First we visited John and Cynthia's farm. When we moved from the city, they were living in a restored house in a fashionable neighbourhood; half their garden was devoted to growing herbs and vegetables for the restaurant they ran on a commercial street a few blocks away. Although their restaurant was a hit with the *beau monde*, they were astute enough to know that fashions change quickly and they could easily end up owning yesterday's chic rendezvous. They had become restless, John especially so. One summer afternoon when they were visiting us, he walked down into the garden after lunch and sat by himself on the grass, watching the warm westerly breeze bend the tops of the poplar trees lining the driveway. That wind was pure oxygen — anything was possible when your lungs were full of it.

He said very little, but I was not surprised when he called and told me they were going to put in an offer on a farm.

"Great!" I exclaimed.

"It's a beef-cattle operation," he said. "It's all set up, you know. There's even a cutting room and a walk-in refrigerator."

"Whuh?"

"You're probably wondering about feed costs. There's about 40 acres in good hay and we'll get all the tractors and tedders and balers, so we'll be self-contained."

"And, uh, where is this farm?"

He named a relatively remote island, with an expensive ferry ride between the farm and the useful farm infrastructure, including the weekly auction, the co-op, and Al the chicken-slaughterer.

My first thought was that he'd gone completely mad, but he wasn't *that* close a friend.

"Sounds wonderful!" I said. "What a piece of Shangri-La! I can't wait to see it."

I had the impression I'd said the right thing, for his voice relaxed and deepened a note or two. It was very Canadian of me to guess what he wanted to hear, rather than tell him the truth. But, on the other hand, if anybody could do it, he and Cynthia could. Their two daughters, who were on either side of the threshold of teenagehood, would adapt well to the island and farm life.

I recalled one time when the whole family had come to visit and the two girls announced they were going to go outside to play. A word from my distant past. "Play" had not seemed to feature in too many children's visits to the farm. "Mope" was common, as was my shouting, "Don't chase the chickens, please!" I told the girls to watch out for the electric fence and went back to adult conversation, but a half hour later when we were outside and walking around I spied them in a corner of the garden. They had made up a game, which apparently didn't involve any sort of mayhem or require any battery-powered gizmos. Nor had they asked where the TV was or whether we had any videos. I liked them a lot.

The next time I saw John a month had passed since his phone call. I was chatting with the sheep when I saw his Volkswagen Westphalia round the corner from the main road onto our dead-end street. They'd bought the van to do some family travelling. I wondered whether it — and the concept of family travel — would survive the move to the farm. He left it at the gate and walked up, looking rather agitated.

"I just signed the papers closing the deal and when I drove off the ferry I turned in this direction instead of toward the city. Show me your place — tell me it's going to be all right."

So we looked at the sheep and chickens and I talked about critters we hadn't yet bought and, after a coffee and an hour or so of country conversation, he happily got into his van and beat his way back to the city.

They moved in in the spring and we went to see them a few months later. Leaving our truck at the dock, we walked onto the ferry and spent a pleasant couple of hours as it chugged from island to island. I couldn't figure out whether I felt liberated or trapped. Cynthia met us at the ferry slip and the three of us crammed into the cab of a Mazda pickup, sharing the seats with a mat of dog hair. They'd traded in the van. We bumped up a hill, passed a couple of stores and the Legion Hall and were soon on a narrow road winding through forest on the way to the south end of the island. A few farms dotted the landscape, but most of the homes looked like summer cottages. It was a charming piece of countryside, a place to establish the farm of your dreams.

"John's fencing," Cynthia told us. "He's hired a local kid, but just for the morning, so we'll see him at lunch."

"Posts and wire?" I asked.

"We need barbed wire for the bull's paddock, but the rest

is field and farm. We're thinning out our woodlot and making our own posts."

"How big's the woodlot?" I pictured a grove.

"It's 30 acres," she said. Three times the size of our farm. "Do you know anything about woodlot management?"

The house stood on a bluff, backed up against their own woods, its windows offering a view across rolling pasture toward a gap in the hills where a small, rocky beach in a cove effected the transition from farmland to sea. Some Hereford cows moved about in the distance. We had lunch and were given the grand tour. They had plans to turn the unfinished basement into a commercial kitchen for a canning operation. One of their new neighbours had said that the Japanese grew tomatoes on the farm in the 1930s, so maybe they'd make their own salsa or a tomato sauce and sell it at the country fairs.

Walking through the fields, we attracted the attention of the herd. A few of the old cows moved away, while the young steers, being fattened for market, bounded up and danced about. Five-hundred-pound playmates. Behind the house, they had a coop with a dozen Heinz 57 chickens pecking about inside; because of the raccoons, they couldn't let their chickens wander loose. They asked us for advice about chickens — we were, after all, more expert than they, but I had the impression, watching them and sensing their strength and enthusiasm, that they would soon know more than we did. Like Richard and Maureen, they had thrown everything they had into their farming adventure and were determined to make a serious go of it. They'd put all their eggs in one basket.

>─┼─◄►─•─O─•─◄►─┼─◄

Our second visit involved a journey into the mountains four hours north of us to see another couple who, coincidentally, had also owned an eatery in the city, a café. But, unlike John and Cynthia, Marianne and Mick had merely "downsized," stuck the surplus money in the bank and were feeling their way onto the rural route.

They had bought a section with an eccentric, self-built house in a narrow river valley running between the mountains. They lived on the edge of pristine wilderness, snowy and cold in the winter, yet hot and dry in the summer. Most of the people who lived there were occupied either with the outdoor-recreation business (skiing, hiking, canoeing, hunting) or the outdoor-desecration business (logging and mining). They had been on the land only a month when a neighbour came by and asked if he could hay their pasture and split the crop with them. Lacking any animals to feed, they got into the hay business. Then Marianne discovered that people were looking for free-range eggs, so they built a coop and on a Saturday drove down to the valley and bought a dozen chickens at the auction. They also bought a breeding pair of rabbits and built a hutch.

Naturally we hadn't seen much of them since we'd left the city and so were pleasantly surprised one day to get a phone call saying they were going to be out our way. We invited them to stop by for a coffee.

"We're doing the café thing all over again," Marianne said. I looked puzzled.

"Well, I mean, I didn't know anything about running a café — I was just a customer there — and one day when I was walking by it had a for-sale sign in the window. And the next thing I knew I'd made an offer on it!"

"Steep learning curve," I acknowledged.

"Right. So tell me about your chickens...."

When they bought the hens at the auction, they'd made the classic error of judging a book by its cover, as it were: the chickens were bright-eyed and well-feathered, but were more or less post-menopausal. They did everything a chicken's supposed to do except lay eggs.

Christine dug out a brochure we had picked up for Happy Hens Hatchery and gave it to them. Marianne guessed she could sell about three dozen eggs a day at the roadside, and figured she'd put in an order for 50 hens. Their rabbits were breeding like ... rabbits, and Mick, who had spent his childhood summers with his grandmother on a Saskatchewan farm, was used to the killing and the cutting and did custom orders for local people. Every few weeks, they filled a large cooler in the back of their 4 x 4 with chilled rabbit and took it to the city, then loaded sacks of grain for the return run.

"And we've opened a B & B too!" Marianne announced with a laugh. "There were extra bedrooms upstairs so we figured *why not?* You've got to come and stay with us."

So on a fine day early in the autumn, Christine and I put some extra food out for the chickens and, leaving Mary in charge of the sheep, hit the road. We bypassed the city and climbed into the mountains, navigating through a ski resort and arriving at last in an area of rough cabins, single-wide mobile homes with yards strewn with broken-down trucks and cars, their hoods up awaiting a repair that had never come. It was a destination for people who didn't want to feel fenced in by any sort of convention.

Their place was on the side of the only road through the area. Handmade, brightly painted signs advertised B & B, FREE-RANGE EGGS, TOOLS SHARPENED $2 & UP. A beautiful meadow stretched into the distance, where a narrowing of the valley framed a picturesque collection of buildings belonging to the next farm and a splendid mountain still frosted with last winter's snow. The house rambled over a patch of ground beside an old orchard. There were coops and a big shed for the hay and another smaller building that might once have been a workshop or a garage.

"I might open a store," Marianne said, gesturing toward the old building. "There are a lot of people tucked away along here who do preserves and crafts. It could just be open when it's open. I wouldn't feel like I had to maintain city hours, but the business side of me says, *maybe there's an opportunity here.*"

She and Mick showed us around. A vegetable garden tightly fenced, a pond dug out with a backhoe to accommodate a collection of Rouen ducks, Muscovies like our long-dead Ducky Daddles and some Toulouse and Chinese geese that started a cheerful, honking clatter when just about anything moved. Their 50 Rhode Island Red chickens occupied a big run and a palatial coop made of hand-hewn timbers, where a marvellous array of ramps allowed the chickens to walk with dignity up to the nesting boxes (ours had to jump). Their rabbits were in another fenced area, contained in large cages to keep them from tunnelling out and making a break for it.

Marianne was a little sheepish about the rabbits. "I feel badly about keeping them locked up like this, but it's the only way to do it. Anyway, it's good healthy meat."

Christine, of all people, concurred. "Even when I was in my most vegetarian stage I'd still eat rabbit occasionally," she said. "It's so lean. I grew up on it in Australia — the 'rabbit-o' used to come by and sell them for sixpence a pair."

Although their farm was isolated, at least compared with ours, there was a steady parade of visitors and customers who found themselves passing by as the sun was beginning to set. A couple of Californians who were planning to hike in the area stopped and rented a room. A member of the Church of the Latter Day Hippie, about 25 years old, with dreadlocks and beads, pulled his Volkswagen van off the road and bought a dozen eggs.

"It's interesting living in a community like this," said Marianne. "I'm old enough to be the mother of a lot of the kids around here. They try to scratc h out an existence during the summer and if they can't make it they cut their hair and get jobs in the restaurants at the ski resort for the winter."

She and Mick were getting everything sorted out for the winter so that they could make a long-planned three-month trip to India.

"There are a couple of New Zealanders down the road who've been organic farming all summer," she said. "They want to stay through the winter, but they're living in an uninsulated cabin with no running water, no washing facilities at all. They're going to stay here and look after the animals."

"And I was going to suggest you get some sheep," I said. "Turn that hay of yours into meat and wool."

"Maybe next year. Isn't that what they say about the prairie farms, that it's next-year country?"

"They mean next year it'll be better. For you, it's 'next year will be different'. I like that."

>─┤─◆〉─●─〈◆─├─◅

"Maybe we should get some new animals?" Christine suggested one evening when we were sitting by our woodstove, books open on our laps and perilously little wine left in the bottle, mulling over what to do. "You know, new challenges. You always talked about getting a donkey. Maybe that would amuse you."

"There are some people who say donkeys are good guard animals for sheep, but the ruling opinion says llamas are better."

Anxiety about the safety of the sheep was constant. I'd believed I'd become more casual — more sanguine — about it the longer we lived there, but I was wrong. Predator awareness was a regular item at the meetings of the local sheep association, followed inevitably by testimonials from llama owners who, coincidentally, had llamas for sale. Quite a few farms had guard llamas and it was a delight to see: a flock of sheep heads-down and grazing, with a llama standing among them, its small head alertly swivelling around on its long neck like a periscope. Both llamas and donkeys are renowned for their hatred of members of the canine family, which includes coyotes, and allegedly will kick them to death if they can't chase them away.

"You should go check out llamas and donkeys, then," Christine said. *Keep him busy and out of trouble,* her tone implied.

Although llamas are very fine and beautiful and can easily be tamed, their uses are somewhat limited: guarding, fleece, or pets or pack animals for trekking, their original use in their South American homeland. And they live a long time; you don't see llama chops on the menu at fine restaurants. From my point of view, it would be like buying a big dog as a pet but refusing to let him into the house.

"The llama thing is a bit like a pyramid sales scheme at the moment," I said. "I think there'll be a price crash soon, because there's just not enough demand for all those out there."

"Well, go look at donkeys, then."

"Only if you'll come too."

I looked in vain for a DONKEYS FOR SALE section in the local paper and had to settle for combing through the general livestock ads. There were ads for jack mules (which I guessed would be big and stubborn and as tough as Borax), horses, cows, sheep, miniature horses, goats, pigs, but no donkeys. What I wanted was a jenny, a small grey donkey like Robert Louis Stevenson's Modestine. One year, when a coyote waltzed in and chomped up one of his lambs, Chuck had bought a pair of donkeys at the auction, but he didn't keep them long. All I heard was the occasional *Eee-aww* from his place, until, abruptly, it stopped.

For a long time the classifieds were entirely bereft of donkeys and I had all but lost interest. Then the sharp-eyed Christine spotted an ad:

DONKEY DOWNSIZING!
BREEDER REDUCING HERD

In a what-the-hell kind of mood, we saddled up the pickup and rode a couple of miles to see what was offered.

The property initially seemed densely wooded, but the driveway ended in a forest clearing, with a beaten-up old house on one side and on the other a paddock bordered by a sturdy fence. It was a tableau utterly devoid of donkeys. A large Lab-cross thundered up, unsure whether to bark or wag his tail. There was the sound of a door closing and a moment later a middle-aged man, short and raggedly dressed, hobbled toward us from behind the house. He walked with that side-to-side, tipped-forward, head-and-arms-back motion of the almost-crippled. Too many years of hard manual labour. He'd be the breeder, we both realized, acknowledging it with the exchange of a glance. Wonder how many times he's been kicked lately?

"You'll be here about the donkeys!" he called brightly.

We nodded.

"They're back in the woods there," he jerked his chin in no direction in particular, "but I'll get 'em in so's we doan have to go lookin'."

He put thumb and finger, both the colour of the ground we stood on, in his mouth and blew a piercing whistle, then began a chant: "C'mon now girls. Hey, c'mere now. C'mon now girls...." Turning to us, he announced, "That'll bring 'em for sure." He stooped awkwardly, lifting the lid off a pail of oats and digging some out with a scoop made from a cut-off bleach bottle. As he spoke, some dun and grey shapes materialized among the trees and came trotting across the paddock toward us. "Chow time!" our host cried and emptied the oats into a feeder hung onto the fence.

The bigger of the two made a beeline for the bucket and arrived there a few steps ahead, burying its big muzzle in the grain. The second one, small and grey and, at first glance, the one I thought I could bond with, wheeled around and with a loud and long *Eeee-awww, eeee-awww* began to kick its companion. There was a loud *Whack! Whack!* as, with all its weight on its front hoofs, it fully extended its back ones in a classic mule kick. The hard metal shoes bashed the bigger donkey in the midriff. It took a good half dozen kicks to move it off the feeder. *Eeee-awww, eeee-awww* brayed the triumphant donkey, and buried its head into the oats.

"Oh, she's a great little fighter!" its owner exclaimed.

I was astounded. My mouth dropped open.

"Close your mouth, Michael, or the flies will get in," Christine whispered.

My hand instinctively covered my mouth. Lacking a dental plan since Christine quit her city job, I was naturally defensive of my front teeth.

Recovering my composure, I asked, "I guess when we just have the one and it bonds with the sheep it won't have this competitive urge?" I didn't want to imagine my sheep kicked to death beside the hay feeder by their putative protector.

"Hunh?"

"We...ah...just...want...the one."

"Naah, they're mother'n daughter. Insep'erbull. Naah, they're only fer sale as a pair."

"Okay, okay — I guess there's been a bit of a misunderstanding. We wanted a single donkey that would bond with our flock and graze with them all day."

"Whuh? You can't leave donkeys out on grass like that. They'll founder." Founder is a hoof disease caused by eating too much rich grass.

"Thanks for the show." We walked back and hopped into the truck.

➤ ┤ ◀➤ ⭕ ◀➤ ┤ ◀

Well, there were always rabbits. Known for being less dangerous than donkeys, rabbits might perhaps be a new, yet manageable, challenge for me. The processing — that is, the killing and the cleaning — would be another one of those things I could talk about if I was ever reduced to joining a men's group.

Christine was enthusiastic. "They'll be less dangerous than the donkeys," she said in a comforting voice, imagining the marriage of a rabbit with red wine in an iron pot above a low flame. She was over a scene from her youth when, on an outing in the Australian countryside, her friend had shot a rabbit that they had cooked and eaten. The experience so haunted her that for two decades she had been a vegetarian. Now, as long as she didn't have to participate in the processing, she would supervise the cooking and participate in the feast.

But where to get rabbits? I thought it best to start with a few to eat and then, if that worked out, look for breeding stock. Rabbit was difficult to buy because of the pervasiveness of the Anglo-North American culture of cute bunnies and wascally wabbits, including Bugs, Peter, Br'er, Roger, Easter and Flopsy. In contrast there were the denizens of *Watership Down*, doubtless more realistic according to stories I'd heard of the buck killing and eating his offspring.

The only local person I knew who raised rabbits was Ken, the farmer from whom I bought my grain and straw. He had a deal with a broker that involved producing a couple of hundred rabbits, live weight between four and six pounds, every fortnight; the broker picked them up and trucked them to a plant for processing. I was as curious about his raising rabbits as he was about my raising broiler chickens, a subject he brought up one day when I was over at his place picking up several hundred pounds of grain.

"I hate chickens!" he said.

"Why?"

"They're so messy, so hard to pluck. You know, if you work on a rabbit line you're expected to skin and clean a rabbit in 30 seconds. That's how easy they are to work with."

"We've got a lot of city friends who won't eat rabbit. They say it's too cute, so we can't serve it to guests."

"Chickens *are* better in that regard. Nobody's got much time for them while they're alive. I'm only too eager to help them to the next stage of their karma so they can be reborn as something *valuable*," he said, chuckling.

"It's so hard to get good rabbit. Do you ever sell any of yours?"

"Normally I have trouble making my quota," he said, "but every once in a while I get a few who grow so big I can't ship 'em. They're over the portion size. They're the good ones, actually, because after they get past five pounds or so all the weight they gain is meat."

"Give me a call if that happens," I said. "I might be interested."

Naturally, one day he called to say he had three of them. Big ones, for which he only wanted $20. What a *deal*. When you find rabbit in the store it usually costs about $12 for something that's more bone than bunny. In fact, I was so enthused that I was halfway there before I realized they'd be alive.

Shit.

It was too late to back out, so I made the best of it and manfully loaded them into my chicken cage. Unlike chickens, which are normally almost catatonic on such an occasion, the rabbits were passive and soft and had big eyes and little noses that twitched....

That evening, we prepared the first one as *Lapin St. Hubert*, in a deep pot with wine, garlic and shallots from the garden and ate it with much ceremony. Months passed before we cooked the second one.

I haven't killed any more rabbits and, in fact, the third one is still somewhere in the depths of the deepfreeze under a couple of dozen chickens. Life is complicated enough with the animals we've already got and it was bad for our image to raise anything in a cage.

Even Ken eventually got out of the rabbit business, but it was the feed costs that were killing him. Because he was raising them in cages, he couldn't feed them his own loose grain because it would scatter and attract even more rats than he already had; instead, he had to sell his grain to the mill and buy it back as pelletized feed. In that exchange, all his profit disappeared.

Entrails in the Sunset

Nothing stays the same for long. Before moving to the farm, we had tried to ignore the ceaseless and — to us — purposeless change in our neighbourhood: small houses demolished and rebuilt as bigger ones, gardens dug up for parking lots.

Now the same thing was happening along our road. City people, with horses and other paraphernalia, bought up the properties around us and those bordering the park. Everything got fixed up as a result; white board fences costing $10 a linear foot ran for thousands of yards around the tidy properties. Young, horse-crazy riders paid off their stable and boarding bills with scrapers and paintbrushes, manure shovels and curry combs. The hedges and woods, home to bird and small beast, began to disappear. But they were generally quiet and anti-trail bikes and other noisemakers, despite car alarms (an especially alien presence on our peaceful country road) that whooped like kicked chickens.

The place across the road fixed itself up as a horse-boarding operation and put in a riding ring visible from our terrace through a screen of birch trees. The horses in the fields were beautifully groomed and paraded decoratively in the sunshine. However, the spate of people attracted to the stables attracted in turn an ice-cream truck that came by twice a day, a wonky tape deck playing either the Scott Joplin ragtime theme from the movie *The Sting*, or Stephen Foster's "Camptown Races" ("do dah, do dah"). Then they put in a huge covered arena with a tin roof more suitable to an industrial park and hired a riding instructor who could have won a shouting contest with a Marine Corps drill sergeant.

One day, a woman came out from the city to buy some rose-bushes from Christine and remarked casually, "Do you know your neighbour has a Bengal tiger?" Fortunately it turned out to be about half a mile away, which by my calculation meant at least six pet dogs and three small children on bicycles. It was lodged on a property that appeared to have an indoor pool adjoining its huge log house. I thought perhaps the woman had been hallucinating until Christine pointed to the side of the road one day while driving by. There, sitting in a square of dirt, a tub of water beside it, was the tiger. "Goodness me, it's a tiger!" we both exclaimed, or words to that effect. I nearly drove off the road.

That autumn it was as if we went to bed one night on a farm and awoke in a television sitcom. But, as the leaves turned, the riding instructor quietened down, the ice-cream pedlar went off to his winter job in telephone sales and the farm regained its magic. In the evenings, skeins of migrating geese flew over on their way south. The sun warmed to the ground during the day so that, when the air chilled after sundown, it sucked veils of fog up into the night.

I decided to plough and reseed the final few acres of pasture. Hayfields deteriorate over time and need rejuvenation and the parasite load increases from running the same type of live-stock year after year. You either have to let it go fallow, reseed it, or change (in our case) from sheep to beef. I called Mel and his powerful tractor over to till the fields, then harrowed it and reseeded it myself. All of this left us short of grass for the 40-odd ewes and lambs that were eating like weight lifters.

A call came from a woman who lived on acreage not far away.

"We've got a lot of grass to cut," she said, "and my husband is spending too much time on the rider mower. I hear you've got Romney lambs for sale."

"They're still pretty small. We lamb later than our neighbours," I said. We were, in fact, among the last to lamb in the valley, a feat we accomplished by keeping the ram away from the ewes until late October. I didn't want to participate in the Easter lamb market, and preferred bringing the lambs into a warmer world in March when the grass was growing well. Fresh grass makes better-quality milk than old hay.

"I'd like a dozen, and all boys if you've got them. Not castrated — they grow faster."

"I'll wean them at the end of May, then bring them over." At that stage, when they're eight to 10 weeks old, they weigh about 50 pounds. Over the summer and fall they grow to 100 to 120 pounds, a good size for someone who wants lamb in the freezer for the winter.

On the appointed day, I loaded them all into the back of the pickup and drove the few miles to her place. It was a grand day, lambs peering curiously through the bars of the stock box at the manicured country gentry zipping by in their Beemers and SUVs, a bit of straw blowing out the back onto the road. I loved the looks I was getting: bumpkin, picturesque, rustic, they implied.

I followed the directions to the customer's address and found myself at a beautiful, park-like property on a high hill with a magnificent view over the countryside. In the distance, so far away that you could choose not to see them, the towers of the city shimmered in the haze. From the narrow roadway a gate opened onto a gravel drive, just two ruts with a grass verge that wound through trees to a house on the hillside. On my left was a large run full of hens, with a magnificent rooster presiding over them; on the right, a grassy meadow dotted with mature evergreen trees extended down the hill to a neighbour's ploughed cornfield. It reminded me of my imaginary farm in the days when we still lived in the city. It was the kind of property where you might find a million-dollar home or even, with a few subtle changes in vegetation, a Tuscan villa.

Contrary to my expectations, the house was small and the couple who lived there unpretentious. They were healthy-looking people, probably 70 years old if they were a day. A generation older than us. They opened a gate and I drove into a big pasture.

"Will you stay for coffee?" she asked as I let the truck's tailgate down and wrestled with the lamb-proof closer I had rigged on the back of the stock box. The lambs had gone from being mildly curious to a bit agitated.

I opened the door, grabbed the nearest one by the leg, dragged him to the edge of the precipice, and lifted him down. Realizing he was free he headed for the hills, but he had gone only a few steps before he discovered he was on beautiful, lush grass. He tasted it, trotted a few steps, sniffed at it and began to crop it. The other lambs followed his lead, jumping down from the truck without my assistance. In a few minutes they had fanned out over the veld. Here for a good time, not a long time.

Over coffee, in my nosy way I quizzed them about their property and how they managed it. They were retired and uninterested in maintaining any breeding stock year-round, for they wanted to travel here and there during the winter, sometimes to Hawaii, sometimes the Arizona desert. At other times they just stayed home. But every spring they bought ready-to-lay pullets from a hatchery and as many lambs as they could get; in November, those went to their separate destinies. These owners were producing crops, just as the prairie farmer does his grain or canola.

When I got home, I told Christine about them and we agreed that this was something we might contemplate in our own future. Although I was unsure how we would get the money together to go away for a long time, as a concept it was certainly better than selling the farm when the day came that the work and the year-round commitment seemed crushing.

"We've got to wait for Eliza to die of old age," I said. "It'll be five years or so, but that'll complete the circle."

"That's okay. I'm in no rush."

>━┼◆>━O━<◆┼━<

The sheep weren't the only ones who were aging. I scored high on the back-pain scale, so I resolved to sell some sheep to any good shepherd who came along. A dozen sheep eat about a bale of hay a day in darkest winter, which makes feeding straight-forward, and I knew I could give a dozen pedicures once every few months without pausing to wolf down a handful of Advil.

It didn't take long to make a list of the ewes I ought to cull. There was Snurgle, who had quickly regained every pound she'd lost during her summertime incarceration in the Fat Farm. Mel was right: she was unlikely to earn her keep again. She had no fear of me, as in the old saying "spare the rod and spoil the sheep," and produced only the occasional lamb. But for somebody who wanted a pet and didn't have a ram around to get her into a lather every autumn, she would be perfect.

What about Norah? As one of the original Gang of Five she had been a steady, fecund sheep, producing twins each year and raising them well, teaching them good manners and life-skills along the way. The previous spring she had produced another pair, but the effort had exhausted her. She was at least eight, possibly nine years old, which is getting up there for a sheep.

Indeed, getting up itself was the problem. She had gone into labour in the middle of the night, luckily coinciding with one of my nocturnal visits to the maternity ward. Hunched beneath a blanket, I took up a position on the hay bales inside the barn where I had a clear view. As the first lamb was born I left my perch, wiped its nose and moved it near the ewe's head for the ritual bonding and licking. A few minutes later she delivered a second one but then lay very still, not raising her head from the straw. I thought she was going to die before my eyes.

Fortunately she was only too tired to stand, and soon lifted her head and began to lick the two blinking, sniffling babies, murmuring in response to their almost-human cries. I went back to my post on the bales, waiting for the two to stand and try to feed. If Norah couldn't get up I'd have to become their wet-nurse, in a manner of speaking.

A half hour passed. The lambs were on their feet and hungry and Norah still didn't get to her feet. Creaking with the cold, I moved the lambs into a small pen and then straddled Norah, putting my hands under her elbows, heaving her front end off the ground and dragging her the 20 feet into the pen. Thank goodness she wasn't a cow. Pulling her up into a sitting position, with her back supported on my thighs and her hind legs flopped out onto the straw, I reached forward, grabbed a lamb, and tried to attach it to one of her teats. The lamb just couldn't get it. I tried the other. Same thing. Sometimes lambs are programmed so strongly to feed with their heads up, as they do when their mother is standing, that they just won't feed from any other position.

I raced back to the house to grab a rubber nipple, a small milk container and a jar that I filled with hot water, making enough noise in the process that Christine awoke and called out, asking if I needed any help. "Not yet," I told her, "you go back to sleep," and I hiked back down to the barn. The two lambs were up and hungry, getting cold, so I had to act fast.

Norah was lying on her side. I crouched in the narrow pen beside her and milked one of her udders into the container. Both lambs began to suck on the edge of my dirty old sweater. I put the nipple on the container, held that in the hot water to warm it, and put a clean finger into one lamb's mouth. It sucked and sucked on my dry "teat."

When I replaced my finger with the nipple, the lamb instantly got a hit of the warm milk, braced its hooves, leaned back and drained the container in seconds. Meanwhile, lamb number 2 got some practice with the finger. I quickly milked Norah's second udder and fed her, then repeated the process until her udders were dried out and both lambs, properly fed and warm, had curled up against her. When I returned to the house and crawled into bed I felt as chilly as the iceberg that woke the passengers on the *Titanic*. Christine muttered, "God, you're cold," and threw an arm, heavy with sleep, over me. I don't think I warmed up till midmorning, but it was more than a day before Norah was able to get up and feed her lambs without my assistance.

I had come close to a classic shepherd's disaster, with a dead ewe and two bottle lambs, and I resolved not to let Norah breed again. To pass her final years with some dignity she needed a job elsewhere as a lawn mower, so I added her to the cull list.

I called John and Cynthia who, during our visit to their island farm, had expressed some interest in having a few sheep to clean up the corners and cut the grass. Bad timing, they said, and if they were to get sheep they'd probably want to jump in with both feet and get some breeding stock. I phoned Jan and asked him to refer to me anybody who was looking for a pet or two. He was skeptical.

"They don't do well if you don't breed them. Coming into heat repeatedly demoralizes them," he said.

"I know, I know, but they're no use for that. They'll just have to suffer."

"If you take them to the auction, they only suffer for the day," he replied matter-of-factly.

I just couldn't do that, so I put an ad in the sheep newspaper under EMPLOYMENT WANTED and finally got a taker: Bill, the neighbour with the draught horses, who hated cutting his grass. Then Chuck and Angela bought a few of our breeding ewes, so that reduced us to 14. Mary, the leader of the flock, became the last survivor of the Gang of Five.

Down at the henhouse, Dave the blond rooster had grown into his role as Cock of the Walk. As the memory faded of his oppression under Arthur's iron spurs, he strutted more boldly and became the sort of take-charge chicken you need when you've got a flock of 25 or 30 hens and a sky full of eagles. Although Dave never mustered the courage to take on Jethro the goose, he had no trouble dominating Arthur's son, the little Barred Rock chick who hatched in the incubator shortly after Arthur's death and grew up to be the spitting image of his dad. The Animal Naming Committee was obviously having a bad day, as this new rooster was known only as Young Arthur. Both of them lived on, scrapping occasionally while taking turns with the diverse collection of hens.

The combination of Dave's handsome blondness and the black-and-white stripes of the Barred Rock hens created some exquisite hybrid hens, feathered in a base colour and a contrasting shade of "pencilling" outlining each feather's edge. On the prettiest chickens, the colouring varied from dark brown with blond pencilling around the tail to almost completely blond at the head. With their bright red combs and wattles, they were the most beautiful chickens I'd ever seen. Unfortunately, because they were hybrids they wouldn't "breed true," so I was unable to make my fortune creating a new breed of chicken. They were excellent mothers, docile and loyal to their chicks, for whom I easily found homes in flocks like Sharon's and Karen's, where aesthetics were as important as production levels.

Lucky the rooster died at age five of some sort of jaundice or cancer, as did Ben, the other survivor among Arthur's early offspring. Both Jan and Sharon moved on to new generations of chickens, and Sharon didn't find any new broilers to save from the roadside ditches.

Favey, the Black Orpington hen who lost the sight in one eye, at one point could only turn left (like an old-fashioned Indy car). With her swollen closed eye and aged, grey face, she looked like a goner. I almost had the hole dug and the hatchet sharpened to put her out of her misery, but then her eye reopened and I surmised that she had been pecked by one of the other hens, probably in a dispute over a worm. Soon she regained her comb and wattle colour, and with a fresh set of feathers following her annual moult she looked almost as good as new.

This created a minor conundrum, for I had painted her likeness and her dates — "1993-1999" — on a ceramic tile that Sharon had fired for me in the kiln at her school. Favey was to be one of the "Great Critters of Killara Farm" series of hand-painted tiles that I would sell for a fortune in my old age to finance our sojourn at the nursing home. As 1999 crept to its end and Favey emerged from the henhouse with a spring in her step every morning, I was forced to contemplate either killing her or breaking the tile. (In art school, I had been influenced by a story of a German symbolist who, when painting a canvas of his backyard, had left out one of the trees due to laziness or perhaps a desire to improve the composition. He had become obsessed with the inaccuracy of his painting, and had cut down the tree.) Being comparatively indecisive, I failed to do anything, so both tile and chicken made it through to the new year.

Jethro and Bev continued to bumble along, incapable of hatching goslings regardless of the money we spent on counselling and videos. Then Christine had a brainwave: the reason they were so noisy, she surmised, and had so much difficulty with mating and parenthood, was because there weren't enough of them to form into a flock! She put in an order for another three pairs of flocking geese, this time from a reputable goose dealer.

Gretchen the barn cat became almost completely dependent on store-bought food, but still would not allow herself to be petted unless she was up to her whiskers in wet cat food. Unlike wild youth who become tame as they get older, she wasn't about to change.

Joyce the ancient duck and her two surviving sons continued to spend most of their time on the pond consorting with the wild things, only coming into the barnyard to freeload when I fed the hens.

As for our own firstborn, Sarah Jane, she came back after a few years of studying at a distant, urban university to find that she liked the farm and animals and didn't think we were so crazy after all. Mind you, she didn't want to move out of the city herself. She was just in her 20s, of course, and true wisdom never arrives until you're somewhat older.